MATERIALS ON INTERNATIONAL HUMAN RIGHTS AND U.S. CRIMINAL LAW AND PROCEDURE

HURST HANNUM

with the collaboration of
Richard B. Lillich
and Stephen A. Saltzburg

The Procedural Aspects of International Law Institute
Washington, DC
1989

ISBN 0-9615124-2-3

TABLE OF CONTENTS

PREFACE

Since its establishment in 1965, the Procedural Aspects of International Law Institute has developed a special interest and expertise in the area of international human rights. Under its first major grant, from the Ford Foundation, it funded the research for and publication of the seventh volume in the "PAIL Series" of monographs, J. Carey, *UN Protection of Civil and Political Rights* (1970). In the ensuing twenty years, the Institute has supported research which has led to publication of, *inter alia*, *Humanitarian Intervention and the United Nations* (R. Lillich ed. 1973); R. Lillich and F. Newman, *International Human Rights: Problems of Law and Policy* (1979); *U.S. Ratification of the Human Rights Treaties: With or Without Reservations?* (R. Lillich ed. 1981); *Guide to International Human Rights Practice* (H. Hannum ed. 1984); D. Harris, *The European Social Charter* (1984); R. Falk, *Reviving the World Court* (1986); H. Hannum, *The Right to Leave and Return in International Law and Practice* (1987); and H. Hannum, *Autonomy, Sovereignty, and Self-Determination* (1989). In 1978, the Institute founded and for five years directed the International Human Rights Law Group, an activist human rights organization based in Washington, DC.

The present work is the second book by the PAIL Institute to analyze international human rights standards and U.S. law in a format designed to be useful to both academics and practitioners. The first, H. Hannum, *Materials on International Human Rights and U.S. Constitutional Law*, was published by the Institute in 1985 and remained, until the present volume, the only serious attempt to compare the substantive law of international and U.S. human rights.

Research and publication of *Materials on International Human Rights and U.S. Criminal Law and Procedure* has been made possible by grants from the Ford Foundation and the Jacob Blaustein Institute for Human Rights, both of which also supported the Institute's study on constitutional law. The materials were prepared by Hurst Hannum, the Institute's Executive Director, with the advice and assistance of the Institute's President, Richard B. Lillich, Howard W. Smith Professor of Law at the University of Virginia, and Professor Stephen A. Saltzburg, author of *American Criminal Procedure* (2d ed. 1984) and currently Deputy Assistant Attorney General, Criminal Division, in the U.S. Department of Justice. Research assistance was provided by Jeff Abbey, University of Virginia School of Law.

The materials were discussed at a small conference of criminal law professors and practitioners, convened by the Institute in June 1988, which contributed significantly to improving the initial draft. We also are grateful for the written comments of Morgan Cloud, Sandra Coliver, James Haddad, and Michael O'Boyle, which enabled us to clarify several initially murky areas. Of course, none of those persons who gave so generously of their time should be held responsible for any errors or omissions which may have found their way into the final product.

As noted in the first section, U.S. courts have only rarely considered international law directly relevant to U.S. standards of criminal due process. However, lawyers, criminologists, and sociologists have long evidenced an interest in comparative systems of criminal justice that goes well beyond the possible application of foreign or international law in a U.S. courtroom. It is hoped that the present work will contribute to that comparison and render more accessible the international perspective that should be a part of every education, both within and outside law schools and universities.

Richard B. Lillich
President, Procedural Aspects of
International Law Institute

Charlottesville, Virginia
March 1989

INTRODUCTION

A system of criminal justice is fundamental to every organized society, and each such system contains unique elements suited to the moral and political values of that society. Formal punishment of an individual who transgresses societal norms is one of the most direct ways in which government affects the individual, perhaps second only to requiring citizens to fight a war.

U.S. criminal law and procedure have been developing slowly and fitfully over two centuries, but international human rights law is a much more recent creation. While the phrase "due process" does not appear in international legal instruments, the concepts of due process and equal protection infuse the substance of these international standards. An essential component of all the relevant international treaties is a concern for fairness in the criminal justice system and ensuring that individual liberty cannot be arbitrarily restrained by the government.[1]

While many rights of the accused, in particular the right of access to a court to challenge detention, are set forth in some detail in international instruments, multilateral treaties which apply globally or even regionally are of necessity much more general than domestic statutes. International human rights law is intended to be applicable and relevant to the entire range of the world's legal systems, encompassing not only the common and civil law traditions but also socialist, Islamic, and other systems which might view the relationship between the individual and the society in very different terms.

The present study identifies and compares norms of U.S. criminal procedure with these basic international instruments. Whether or not it is possible to invoke international law directly in domestic litigation,[2] wider

---

[1]The materials which follow are concerned with international human rights law related to the criminal process, and not with "international criminal law" per se. The latter involves issues such as individual responsibility for acts designated as international crimes (e.g., genocide, terrorism) and the appropriate reach of domestic and international jurisdiction over such crimes. *See generally* M.C. BASSIOUNI, INTERNATIONAL CRIMINAL LAW (1980).

[2]*See* discussion *infra* at 2–12.

knowledge of the substance of international law should be of interest to those seeking legislative and administrative reform in the U.S. criminal justice system, as well as those who have a more scholarly interest in the process. Given that international human rights law establishes only minimum standards in most instances, the present materials focus on U.S. constitutional requirements, rather than state or federal criminal law. While a comparative survey such as the present work cannot hope even to mention many of the major issues which will be familiar to American criminal law experts,[3] it is hoped that it will give some content to the developing international right to liberty and to a fair trial, thereby providing a point of comparison with U.S. jurisprudence.

Impact of International Human Rights Law in U.S. Courts

The Treaty Power

Under article VI, section 2, of the U.S. Constitution, "all Treaties made, or which shall be made, under the Authority of the United States, shall be the supreme Law of the Land; and the Judges in every State shall be bound thereby, any Thing in the Constitution or Laws of any State to the Contrary notwithstanding." It is well-established that a self-executing treaty[4] (or a non-self-executing treaty implemented by Congress) supersedes prior inconsistent federal statutes[5] as well as all inconsistent state and local laws.[6]

Although the Supreme Court has stated that the subject matter of treaties is limited "to all proper subjects of negotiation between our government and the governments of other nations,"[7] neither this oft-quoted phrase nor subsequent cases suggest any significant limitations on the matters that the President and Senate may appropriately address by treaty.[8] The only agreed exceptions to this power are those acts that are specifically reserved in the Constitution to Congress or the President,

---

[3]For example, a leading treaties on criminal procedure identifies 17 distinct steps in the processing of a "typical" criminal case. *See* W.R. LAFAVE & J.H. ISRAEL, CRIMINAL PROCEDURE (student ed. 1985 & Supp. 1987), at 7–19.

[4]*See* text at notes 11–19 *infra*.

[5]*See, e.g.*, Cook v. United States, 288 U.S. 102, 118–19 (1933); AMERICAN LAW INSTITUTE, RESTATEMENT (THIRD) OF THE FOREIGN RELATIONS LAW OF THE UNITED STATES § 115(2) (1987) [hereinafter cited as "RESTATEMENT"]. Reciprocally, under the "last-in-time" rule, a subsequently enacted inconsistent statute will prevail over an earlier self-executing treaty. *See, e.g.*, Whitney v. Robertson, 124 U.S. 190, 194 (1888); RESTATEMENT § 115(1)(a).

[6]*See, e.g.*, Asakura v. Seattle, 265 U.S. 332, 341 (1924); RESTATEMENT § 115 comment e at 66.

[7]Geofroy v. Riggs, 133 U.S. 258, 266 (1890).

[8]Rejecting the argument that a treaty must deal with "a matter of international concern," whatever that phrase may mean, the *Restatement* concludes that "the United States may make an agreement on any subject suggested by its national interests in relations with other nations." RESTATEMENT § 302 comment c at 154.

e.g., the power to tax or to declare war, and therefore cannot be accomplished directly by treaty.[9]

Customary international law being federal common law,[10] it automatically is applicable in cases where it is relevant. Early on, however, the Supreme Court held that it was only when a treaty is self-executing, "whenever it operates of itself without the aid of any legislative provision,"[11] that it may be directly relied upon for the enforcement of rights. There being no international rule as to whether a treaty is domestically enforceable, U.S. domestic law determines whether a treaty is self-executing, i.e., potentially giving rise to directly enforceable rights,[12] or non-self-executing, i.e., not creating directly enforceable rights in the absence of Congressional implementing legislation.

There is much disagreement as to the criteria that should be considered in determining whether or not a treaty is self-executing, and the Fifth Circuit Court of Appeals has referred to the question of self-execution as "one of the most confounding in treaty law."[13] In spite of a relatively early Supreme Court admonition that "[t]reaties are to be construed in a broad and liberal spirit, and, when two constructions are possible, one restrictive of rights that may be claimed under it and the other favorable to them, the latter is to be preferred,"[14] lower courts in the United States have fairly consistently refused to hold that multilateral human rights treaties are self-executing and thus potentially directly enforceable.[15] Only the Protocol Relating to the Status of Refugees (among such multilateral treaties) has been viewed as having some effect on individual rights.[16]

---

[9] *Id.* § 111 comment i at 47–48 and Reporters' Note 6 at 56–57.

[10] RESTATEMENT § 111 comment d at 44 and Reporters' Note 3 at 50.

[11] Foster v. Nielson, 27 U.S. (2 Pet.) 253, 314 (1829). *Accord* Whitney v. Robertson, *supra* note 5; Dreyfus v. Von Finck, 534 F.2d 24, 30 (2d Cir.), *cert. denied*, 429 U.S. 835 (1976).

[12] "Whether a treaty is self-executing is a question distinct from whether the treaty creates private rights or remedies," RESTATEMENT § 111 comment h at 47, and not all self-executing treaties confer directly enforceable rights upon private parties. *See id.* § 907 comment a at 395 and Reporters' Note 1 at 397 (citing the Head Money Cases, 112 U.S. 580, 598–99 (1884)).

[13] United States v. Postal, 589 F.2d 862, 876 (5th Cir.), *cert. denied*, 444 U.S. 832 (1979). *See* Riesenfeld, *The Doctrine of Self-Executing Treaties and U.S. v. Postal: Win at Any Price?*, 74 AM. J. INT'L L. 892 (1980); *cf.* Paust, *Self-Executing Treaties*, 82 *id.* 760 (1988) (arguing that all treaties should be presumed to be self-executing, with very limited exceptions). Perhaps the best judicial attempt at identifying the criteria for determining whether or not a treaty is self-executing is People of Saipan ex rel. Guerrero v. U.S. Dep't of Interior, 502 F.2d 90 (9th Cir. 1974), *cert. denied*, 420 U.S. 1003 (1975).

[14] Asakura v. Seattle, *supra* note 6, at 342.

[15] *See, e.g.*, Doe v. Plyler, 628 F.2d 448, 453 (5th Cir. 1980) (OAS Charter); Sei Fujii v. State, *infra* note 17, at 722–25 (UN Charter). But compare *People of Saipan*, *supra* note 13 (U.S.-UN Trusteeship Agreement held to be self-executing).

[16] The self-executing nature of many of the provisions of the Protocol, *signed* 31 Jan. 1967, *entered into force* for U.S. 1 Nov. 1968, 19 U.S.T. 6223, T.I.A.S. No. 6577, *reprinted in* R. LILLICH, INTERNATIONAL HUMAN RIGHTS INSTRUMENTS 110.1 (1988), which incorporates by reference the

Although the case never was appealed to the U.S. Supreme Court, the holding by the California Supreme Court in *Sei Fujii v. State*[17] that the human rights clauses of the UN Charter were non-self-executing has been followed with little discussion or analysis by state and federal courts since 1952.[18] While some commentators suggest that the case might be decided differently today, particularly in view of the greater specificity that international "human rights" have acquired since adoption of the Charter, no case to date has explicitly departed from the *Fujii* holding.[19]

As a practical matter, the self-executing versus non-self-executing distinction is perhaps less important than it might appear, given the poor record of U.S. ratification of international human rights treaties. Moreover, each of the five major treaties submitted by President Carter to the Senate for ratification in 1978 came with a suggested declaration to the effect that it was to be considered non-self-executing,[20] as did the Convention Against Torture submitted by President Reagan in 1988.[21] Thus the likelihood of courts in the United States finding that international human rights treaties are self-executing, much less that they create directly enforceable rights, seems fairly remote at present.

Customary International Law

Although customary international law is not specifically mentioned in the Constitution, the Supreme Court has declared that it also is "part of

---

Convention Relating to the Status of Refugees, *signed* 28 July 1951, *entered into force* 22 Apr. 1954, 189 U.N.T.S. 137, *reprinted in* LILLICH, *id.*, at 280.1, has been assumed *sub silentio* by several lower courts, although the U.S. Immigration and Naturalization Service took the position that U.S. ratification of the Protocol required no change in existing U.S. law or practice. In any event, U.S. refugee law was brought more in line with international norms by enactment of the Refugee Act of 1980, now codified at 8 U.S.C. § 1101 *et seq.* (1988). The Supreme Court subsequently upheld the proposition that current U.S. law and practice are consistent with the provisions of the Protocol. I.N.S. v. Stevic, 467 U.S. 407, 417-18 (1984). Many bilateral treaties affecting individual rights have been enforced directly with little judicial discussion. *See generally* RESTATEMENT § 111 comments h and i at 46-48 and Reporters' Notes 5 and 6 at 53-57.

[17]38 Cal. 2d 718, 242 P.2d 617 (1952).

[18]For arguments to the effect that the human rights clauses of the UN Charter – or at least the basic nondiscrimination norm contained in Article 55(c) – are self-executing, see Lillich, *infra* note 28, at 371-85.

[19]For a recent decision holding that the UN Charter's human rights clauses are non-self-executing and hence "do not confer rights on individual citizens," see Frolova v. U.S.S.R., 761 F.2d 370, 374 (7th Cir. 1985).

[20]Message of the President Transmitting Four Treaties Pertaining to Human Rights, S. Exec. Doc. Nos. C, D, E & F, 95th Cong., 2d Sess. viii, xi, xv, xviii (1978); Message of the President Transmitting the Convention on the Elimination of All Forms of Discrimination Against Women, S. Exec. Doc. No. R, 96th Cong., 2d Sess. ix (1980). Although the Senate Foreign Relations Committee held informational hearings on the first four treaties in 1979, International Human Rights Treaties: Hearings Before the Senate Comm. on Foreign Relations, 96th Cong., 1st Sess. (1979), it has taken no action on them. *See generally* U.S. RATIFICATION OF THE HUMAN RIGHTS TREATIES: WITH OR WITHOUT RESERVATIONS? (R. Lillich ed. 1981).

[21]Message of the President Transmitting the Convention Against Torture and Other Cruel, Inhuman or Degrading Treatment or Punishment, S. Treaty Doc. No. 20, 100th Cong., 2d Sess. 2 (1988).

our law, and must be ascertained and administered by the courts of justice of appropriate jurisdiction, as often as questions of right depending upon it are duly presented for their determination."[22] As in the case of treaties, customary international law supersedes all inconsistent state and local laws[23] and, although this issue has not been judicially resolved, perhaps prior inconsistent federal statutes and international agreements as well.[24]

The content of customary international law is determined in large measure by reference to state practice, which includes, *inter alia*, "diplomatic acts and instructions as well as public measures and other governmental acts and official statements of policy, whether they are unilateral or undertaken in cooperation with other states. . . ."[25] Widely ratified human rights treaties, such as the International Covenant on Civil and Political Rights,[26] also may contribute to the creation of specific human rights recognized under customary international law,[27] although not every right mentioned in such treaties rises to the status of customary, and therefore binding, international law.[28] So, too, may resolutions of international organizations, such as the UN's Universal Declaration of Human Rights,[29] national and international judicial and arbitral decisions,[30] and the opinions of prominent scholars.[31]

---

[22]The Paquete Habana, 175 U.S. 677, 700 (1900). The Court added the important (and often overlooked) caveats that customary international law is applicable only in cases "where there is no treaty, *and no controlling executive or legislative act* or judicial decision," and "in the absence of any treaty *or other public act of their own government* in relation to the matter." *Id.* at 700, 708 (emphasis added). Relying on these caveats, the Eleventh Circuit recently gave effect to the Attorney General's action authorizing the continued detention of undocumented aliens despite its recognition that such detention violated customary international law. Garcia-Mir v. Meese, 788 F.2d 1446, 1453 (11th Cir.), *cert. denied*, 479 U.S. 889 (1986). *Compare* text at notes 34 & 44 *infra*.

[23]RESTATEMENT § 111(1) and § 115 comment e at 66.

[24]*Id.* § 115 Reporters' Note 4 at 68. *Compare* Henkin, *International Law as Law in the United States*, 82 MICH. L. REV. 1555, 1561–67 (1984) (customary international law may supersede prior inconsistent federal statute) *with* Goldklang, *Back on Board the Paquete Habana: Resolving the Conflict Between Statutes and Customary International Law*, 25 VA. J. INT'L L. 143 (1984) (contra).

[25]RESTATEMENT § 102(2) comment b at 25. *See generally* A. D'AMATO, THE CONCEPT OF CUSTOM IN INTERNATIONAL LAW (1971); C. PARRY, THE SOURCES AND EVIDENCES OF INTERNATIONAL LAW (1965).

[26]Note 74 *infra*.

[27]RESTATEMENT § 102(3) comment i at 27 and Reporters' Note 5 at 33–34. On the role of treaties in the creation of the customary international law of human rights, *compare* Weisburd, *Customary International Law: The Problem of Treaties*, 21 VAND. J. TRANSNAT'L L. 1 (1988) (treaties relatively unimportant) *with* D'Amato, *Custom and Treaty: A Response to Professor Weisburd*, 21 *id.* 459 (1988) (treaties exceptionally important).

[28]*See* Lillich, *Invoking International Human Rights Law in Domestic Courts*, 54 U. CIN. L. REV. 367, 400 n.156, 402 n.165 (1985). *Cf.* Higgins, *Derogations Under Human Rights Treaties*, 48 BRIT. Y.B. INT'L L. 281, 282 (1976–77).

[29]Note 73 *infra*. *See* RESTATEMENT § 103 comment c at 37 and Reporters' Note 2 at 38–39.

[30]RESTATEMENT § 103(2)(a) & (b).

[31]*Id.* § 103 Reporters' Note 1 at 37–38. These opinions may be ascertained from their writings or by affidavits or expert testimony in a particular case. *Id.* § 113 comment c at 61 and Reporters' Note 1 at 61–62. See Filartiga v. Peña-Irala, *infra* note 36, at 879 & n.4 (affidavits), and Fernandez-Roque v. Smith, *infra* note 34, at 902 (expert testimony).

The *Restatement (Third) of the Foreign Relations Law of the United States*, which falls under the last category, identifies genocide; slavery; murder or "causing the disappearance" of individuals; torture or other cruel, inhuman or degrading treatment or punishment; prolonged arbitrary detention; systematic racial discrimination; and consistent patterns of gross violations of internationally recognized human rights as violations of customary international law.[32] During this decade, U.S. courts have held that torture,[33] prolonged arbitrary detention[34] and "causing the disappearance" of individuals[35] are prohibited by the customary international law of human rights.

The well-reasoned opinion of the Second Circuit in *Filartiga v. Peña-Irala*[36] referred, *inter alia*, to the Universal Declaration of Human Rights,[37] the UN's 1975 Declaration on Torture,[38] and regional human rights treaties in arriving at its determination that torture violated "the law of nations" within the meaning of the Alien Tort Claims Act.[39] While *Filartiga*'s significance in defining either the scope or content of customary international law should not be overestimated,[40] it is a seminal decision and an important demonstration of how to prove customary international human rights law.[41]

Perhaps as significant was the decision of the U.S. District Court for the District of Kansas in *Fernandez v. Wilkinson*,[42] which considered

---

[32]RESTATEMENT § 702. Indeed, it regards the above norms not only to be customary international law, but also *jus cogens* (rendering international agreements violating them void). *Id.* § 702 comment n at 167 and Reporters' Note 11 at 174. On this and other aspects of Section 702, see Lillich, *Remarks*, 79 AM. SOC'Y INT'L L. PROC. 84 (1985).

[33]*See, e.g.*, Filartiga v. Peña-Irala, *infra* note 36, at 884.

[34]*See, e.g.*, Fernandez-Roque v. Smith, 622 F. Supp. 887, 903 (N.D. Ga. 1985), *rev'd in part & aff'd in part & dismissed as moot in part sub nom.* Garcia-Mir v. Meese, 788 F.2d 1446, 1453 (11th Cir.), *cert. denied*. 479 U.S. 889 (1986).

[35]*See* Forti v. Suarez-Mason, 694 F. Supp. 707, 711 (N.D. Cal. 1988).

[36]Filartiga v. Peña-Irala, 630 F.2d 876 (2d Cir. 1980).

[37]Note 73 *infra*.

[38]Declaration on the Protection of All Persons from being Subjected to Torture and Other Cruel, Inhuman or Degrading Treatment or Punishment, *adopted* 9 Dec. 1975, G.A. Res. 3452, 30 U.N. GAOR Supp. (No. 34) at 91, U.N. Doc. A/1034 (1975), *reprinted in* R. LILLICH, *supra* note 16, at 480.1.

[39]Judiciary Act, ch. 20, § 9, 1 Stat. 73, 77 (1789) (codified at 28 U.S.C. 1350 (1988)).

[40]*Compare* Hanoch Tel-Oren v. Libyan Arab Republic, 517 F. Supp. 542 (D.D.C. 1981), *aff'd per curiam*, 726 F.2d 774 (D.C. Cir. 1984), *cert. denied*, 470 U.S. 1003 (1985).

[41]For a demonstration of how to prove the existence of customary international human rights law, see Hartman, *"Unusual" Punishment: The Domestic Effects of International Norms Restricting the Application of the Death Penalty*, 52 U. CIN. L. REV. 655, 665–86 (1983). The articles by Weisburd and D'Amato cited in note 27 *supra* consider the proper role of human rights treaties in this process.

[42]Fernandez v. Wilkinson, 505 F. Supp. 787 (D. Kan. 1980), *aff'd on other grounds sub nom.* Rodriguez-Fernandez v. Wilkinson, 654 F.2d 1382 (10th Cir. 1981).

whether the continued detention of a Cuban who had arrived in the United States in 1980 as part of the "freedom flotilla" violated domestic or international law. After finding that the plaintiff's unique status as an "excludable" alien meant that he could not avail himself of constitutional or statutory protections, the District Court nevertheless ordered his release.

> Our review of the sources from which customary international law is derived clearly demonstrates that arbitrary detention is prohibited by customary international law. Therefore, even though the indeterminate detention of an excluded alien cannot be said to violate the United States Constitution or our statutory laws, it is judicially remedial as a violation of international law.[43]

On appeal, the Tenth Circuit affirmed the District Court's order, but based its holding on U.S. statutory provisions rather than on international law. The Court of Appeals nevertheless found it proper "to consider international law principles for notions of fairness" and noted that its interpretation of the relevant statute "is consistent with accepted international law principles."[44]

The above two cases applied customary international law either where explicitly directed to by statute (*Filartiga*) or to interpret essentially consistent (if incomplete) federal law (*Fernandez v. Wilkinson*). Where invalidation of a state law was sought, however, the U.S. District Court for the Southern District of Texas found that "the right to education, while it represents an important international goal, has not acquired the status of customary international law."[45] The District Court's discussion of the international law issues was confused, at best, although it apparently assumed *sub silentio* that customary international law would be controlling were it proved.[46]

Although it did not address the domestic impact of international human rights law, the position taken by the United States in the *Hostages Case*[47] before the International Court of Justice recognized the international legal obligation of nations to observe certain minimum standards in their treatment of aliens and noted the duty of every country to respect "certain fundamental human rights" as evidenced, *inter alia*, by the UN

---

[43]505 F. Supp. at 798.

[44]654 F.2d at 1388, 1390. *But see* Jean v. Nelson, 727 F.2d 957, 974–75 (11th Cir. 1984) (en banc), *aff'd*, 472 U.S. 846 (1985), where the Eleventh Circuit specifically declined to follow the Tenth Circuit's reasoning in *Rodriguez-Fernandez*. The Supreme Court did not resolve the split. *Cf. Garcia-Mir v. Meese*, *supra* note 22.

[45]In re Alien Children Litigation, 501 F. Supp. 544, 596 (S.D. Tex. 1980), *aff'd sub nom*. Plyler v. Doe, 457 U.S. 202 (1982).

[46]For a critique of the District Court's opinion, see Lillich, *supra* note 28,at 406–08.

[47]Case Concerning United States Diplomatic and Consular Staff in Tehran (U.S. v. Iran), 1980 I.C.J. 3.

Charter, the Universal Declaration of Human Rights, and the International Covenant on Civil and Political Rights.[48]

The U.S. Supreme Court has neither welcomed nor criticized references to international human rights law by lower courts in recent years. In several cases this decade in which it might have referred to international law as supportive of or consistent with controlling statutory or constitutional principles, it has rested its decisions solely on domestic grounds.[49]

Federal Laws

Despite echoes of the "Bricker Amendment" debate in the 1950s from a few persons who purport to fear that international law may unconstitutionally enlarge the powers of the federal government or abridge constitutionally guaranteed rights, it is clear that no treaty can override or supersede the U.S. Constitution. As the Supreme Court categorically stated in *Reid v. Covert*, "[t]here is nothing in [the Supremacy Clause] which intimates that treaties and laws enacted pursuant to them do not have to comply with the provisions of the Constitution. . . . The prohibitions of the Constitution were designed to apply to all branches of the National Government and they cannot be nullified by the Executive or by the Executive and Senate combined."[50] Whatever international obligations the United States may have under customary or conventional international law, domestically the Constitution prevails.

Since treaties and federal statutes have equal status under the Constitution, the one adopted last has been held to prevail, under the theory that "the last expression of the sovereign will must control."[51] Although the Supreme Court has not considered the issue, at least one lower court has held that some executive agreements may not supersede prior Congressional legislation.[52]

While human rights treaties or customary international law is applied directly by courts in the United States relatively infrequently, there is increasing support for the "indirect incorporation" of international norms

---

[48]Memorial of the Government of the United States of America at 71.

[49]*See* Plyler v. Doe, *supra* note 45 (right to education); Bob Jones Univ. v. United States, 461 U.S. 574 (1983) (racial discrimination); Grove City College v. Bell, 465 U.S. 555 (1984) (sex discrimination).

[50]354 U.S. 1, 16–17 (1957). See RESTATEMENT § 302(2) comment b at 153 and Reporters' Note 1 at 155.

[51]The Chinese Exclusion Case, 130 U.S. 581, 600 (1889). See text at and accompanying note 5 *supra*.

[52]United States v. Guy W. Capps, 204 F.2d 655 (4th Cir. 1953), *aff'd on other grounds*, 348 U.S. 296 (1955) (executive agreement disregarding procedures prescribed by Congress for limiting imports). *Cf.* RESTATEMENT § 115 Reporters' Note 5 at 68–69. For criticism of the tentative draft of the Restatement's treatment of this question, see Note, *Superseding Statutory Law by Sole Executive Agreement: An Analysis of the American Law Institute's Shift in Position*, 23 VA. J. INT'L L. 671 (1983).

to "inform" constitutional and statutory interpretation. As early as 1948, four justices of the Supreme Court cited the UN Charter as additional support for the invalidation of a racially discriminatory alien land law,[53] and there have been frequent references to the Universal Declaration of Human Rights and other international instruments in both federal and state courts.[54] More recently, a majority of the justices of the Supreme Court invoked various international human rights treaty provisions to support their holding that the Eighth and Fourteenth Amendments prohibit the execution of juveniles.[55] Even clearly non-binding instruments such as the UN Standard Minimum Rules for the Treatment of Prisoners have been cited to help define the scope of permissible prison conditions under the Eighth Amendment.[56]

This use of international law to inform constitutional or statutory interpretation is hardly innovative, although the increased use of specific international human rights norms is of more recent vintage. "[A]ny act of congress ought never to be construed to violate the law of nations if any other possible construction remains," ruled the Supreme Court in 1804,[57] and the interpretation of domestic laws in a manner consistent with international obligations is common in most jurisdictions.[58]

It also should be noted that certain international obligations may be imposed upon the United States upon signature of a treaty, even prior to its formal ratification. Pursuant to the Vienna Convention on Treaties, which is widely considered to be expressive of customary international law on the interpretation and effect of international agreements, the United States is under an affirmative obligation not to take any action

---

[53]Oyama v. California, 332 U.S. 633, 649–50 & n.4, 673 (1948) (Black, J. & Douglas, J., concurring; Murphy, J. & Rutledge, J., concurring). For an excellent survey of post-World War II civil rights litigation invoking the human rights clauses of the UN Charter, see Lockwood, *The United Nations Charter and United States Civil Rights Litigation: 1946–1955*, 69 IOWA L. REV. 901 (1984).

[54]*See* cases collected in R. LILLICH, *supra* note 16, at 440.6–440.8.

[55]Thompson v. Oklahoma, *infra* note 307, at 2696 n.34, 2707–08.

[56]*See, e.g.*, Lareau v. Manson, 507 F. Supp. 1177, 1187 n.9 (D. Conn 1980), *aff'd in part & modified in part*, 651 F.2d 96, 106 & n.6, 107 (2d Cir. 1981). Other cases are collected in R. LILLICH, *supra* note 16, at 450.14.

[57]Murray v. Schooner Charming Betsy, 6 U.S. (2 Cranch) 64, 117–18 (1804). *Accord* Lauritzen v. Larsen, 345 U.S. 571, 578 (1953). *See* RESTATEMENT § 114.

[58]In Great Britain, which does not recognize the doctrine of self-executing treaties, "the courts are accustomed to interpreting statute[s] so as to conform with international obligations." D. KEIR & F. LAWSON, CASES IN CONSTITUTIONAL LAW 11 (6th ed. 1979). Canada is in accord. *See* Cohen & Bayefsky, *The Canadian Charter of Rights and Freedoms and Public International Law*, 61 CAN. BAR REV. 265, 295–96 (1983). The Court of Justice of the European Communities has stated that "international treaties on the protection of human rights in which the member-States have co-operated or to which they have adhered can also supply indications which may be taken into account within the framework of Community Law." Firma J. Nold KG v. E.C. Comm'n, 2 Comm. Mkt. L.R. 338, 354 (1974).

contrary to the purpose of a treaty which it has signed, pending ratification.[59]

It is paradoxical that, in an increasingly complex world in which ever greater deference seems to be given to the executive branch in the areas of foreign affairs and national security, federal (and state) judges may be less knowledgeable and aware of international law and its importance than they were 200 years ago.[60] The present materials are most likely to be useful to courts and lawyers in interpreting constitutional and statutory provisions; in only relatively rare instances will customary international law or one of the few international human rights treaties that the United States has ratified have direct application to a case involving individual rights.

Certainly the increasing corpus of international human rights jurisprudence and the United States' formal and informal adherence to human rights norms suggest that such norms are appropriate to consider in interpreting the rights and liberties protected by the Constitution. As the Supreme Court noted nearly 70 years ago, "when we are dealing with words that also are a constituent act, like the Constitution of the United States, we must realize that they have called into life a being the development of which could not have been foreseen completely by the most gifted of its begetters. . . . The case before us must be considered in the light of our whole experience and not merely in that of what was said a hundred years ago."[61]

State Laws and Constitutions

The propensity for courts to find that an international human rights treaty is non-self-executing or that a customary international law norm is insufficiently proven may be understandable when a contrary finding would require "trumping" a federal statute, but no such reluctance should be present when a state or local law rather than a federal statute is challenged. "Though a court will not undertake to construe a treaty in a manner inconsistent with a subsequent federal statute, no similar hesitancy obtains if the asserted clash is with state law."[62] "Plainly, the external powers of the United States are to be exercised without regard to state

---

[59]Vienna Convention on the Law of Treaties, *adopted* 22 May 1969, *entered into force* 27 Jan. 1980, art. 18, 1155 U.N.T.S. 331, 336, *reprinted in* R. LILLICH, *supra* note 16, at 540.2.

[60]*See* Christenson, *Using Human Rights Law to Inform Due Process and Equal Protection Analyses*, 52 U. CIN. L. REV. 3, 6 (1983). Earlier this decade the Lawyers Committee for International Human Rights and the Aspen Institute conducted a series of seminars designed to educate federal judges on international human rights law issues. Such efforts should be revived and expanded to include state judges.

[61]Missouri v. Holland, 252 U.S. 416, 433 (1920).

[62]Baker v. Carr, 369 U.S. 186, 212 (1962).

laws or policies. . . . [C]omplete power over international affairs is in the national government and is not and cannot be subject to any curtailment or interference on the part of the several states."[63] "[S]tate law must yield when it is inconsistent with, or impairs the policy or provisions of, a treaty or of an international compact or agreement. Then, the power of a State to refuse enforcement of rights based on foreign law which runs counter to the public policy of the forum . . . must give way before the superior Federal policy evidenced by a treaty or international compact or agreement."[64]

In addition to invalidation of a state or local law by the direct operation of a treaty or customary international law through the Supremacy Clause, state action also may constitute an unconstitutional encroachment upon even unexercised federal powers in the foreign affairs area. In *Zschernig v. Miller*, the Supreme Court invalidated a state alien inheritance law, despite the absence of a treaty, on the grounds that the law as applied intruded into the field of foreign affairs entrusted to the President and Congress and would require unacceptable judicial inquiry into the actions of foreign governments.[65]

In overturning a state alien registration statute where the federal government had enacted "a complete scheme of [alien] registration," the Supreme Court added that

> it is of importance that this legislation is in a field which affects international relations, the one aspect of our government that from the first has been most generally conceded imperatively to demand broad national authority. . . . And it is also of importance that this legislation deals with the rights, liberties, and personal freedoms of human beings, and is in an entirely different category from state tax statutes or state pure food laws regulating the labels on cans.[66]

More recently, an anti-Iranian regulation adopted by the University of New Mexico at the height of the U.S. hostage crisis was invalidated by a lower court on the grounds that it "imposes an impermissible burden on the federal government's power to regulate immigration and conduct foreign affairs."[67]

Admittedly, such instances of the invalidation of state laws on the

---

[63]United States v. Belmont, 301 U.S. 324, 331 (1937).

[64]United States v. Pink, 315 U.S. 203, 230–31 (1942). Or by customary international law. *See* note 23 *supra*.

[65]389 U.S. 429 (1968). While subsequent lower court opinions have read *Zschernig* narrowly to apply primarily to the impropriety of judicial examination of foreign governments' actions, the basic holding has not been questioned.

[66]Hines v. Davidowitz, 312 U.S. 52, 68 (1941).

[67]Tayyari v. New Mexico State Univ., 495 F. Supp. 1365, 1380 (D.N.M. 1980).

ground of impermissible interference with federal foreign affairs policy have been rare. For example, the Supreme Court did not mention the role of international law or foreign affairs in a decision invalidating a local law in Texas that imposed tuition on undocumented alien elementary school children, despite its obvious relevance to U.S. immigration and foreign affairs policies.[68]

Finally, there is a growing trend on the part of state courts to extend individual rights through the use of state laws and constitutions rather than by reliance upon federal constitutional provisions.[69] Thus, state courts are equally (and perhaps even more) fertile fields for the utilization of international human rights law as a means of informing or interpreting state constitutional or statutory provisions.[70] The Supreme Courts of California and Oregon have referred to international human rights instruments in recent decisions,[71] and the arguments advanced above with respect to informing U.S. constitutional and statutory analyses are equally valid in the state context.[72]

Sources of International Human Rights Law

The domestic impact of human rights treaties and agreements and customary international law is discussed in the immediately preceding section. Where the intent is to influence or guide interpretation of U.S. constitutional provisions, however, the technical status of an international instrument is probably less relevant than its persuasive authority within the realm of international law generally and human rights law in particular.

The most important international instruments, although not necessarily the most detailed, are those adopted under the auspices of the United Nations. The "International Bill of Human Rights" consists of the Universal Declaration of Human Rights;[73] the International Covenant on Civil and Political Rights and the Optional Protocol thereto;[74] and the

---

[68]Plyler v. Doe, *supra* note 45.

[69]*See* Brennan, *The Bill of Rights and the States: The Revival of State Constitutions as Guardians of Individual Rights*, 61 N.Y.U. L. REV. 535 (1986); see also J. NOWAK, R. ROTUNDA & J. YOUNG, CONSTITUTIONAL LAW 20–22 (2d ed. 1983).

[70]*See* Burke, Coliver, de la Vega & Rosenbaum, *Application of International Human Rights Law in State and Federal Courts*, 18 TEX. INT'L L.J. 291 (1983); *Proceedings: Conference on International Human Rights Law in State and Federal Courts*, 17 U.S.F. L. REV. 1 (1982); and *Symposium on International Human Rights Law in State Courts*, 18 INT'L LAW. 59 (1984).

[71]*See, e.g.*, American Nat'l Ins. Co. v. Fair Employment & Hous. Comm'n, 32 Cal. 3d 603, 608 n.4, 651 P.2d 1151, 1154 n.4 (1982); Sterling v. Cupp, 290 Or. 611, 622 n.21, 625 P.2d 123, 131 n.21 (1981).

[72]For an accurate and sympathetic exposition by a prominent state court judge of the difficulties likely to be encountered in the state context, see Linde, *Symposium*, *supra* note 70, at 77–81.

[73]*Signed* 10 Dec. 1948, G.A. Res. 217A, U.N. Doc. A/180, at 71 (1948), *reprinted in* R. LILLICH, *supra* note 16, at 440.1 [hereinafter cited as "UnivDec"].

[74]*Adopted* 16 Dec. 1966, *entered into force* 23 Mar. 1976, 999 U.N.T.S. 171 (1966), *reprinted in* R. LILLICH, *supra* note 16, at 170.1 [hereinafter cited as "CivPol"].

International Covenant on Economic, Social and Cultural Rights.[75] The two Covenants are considered the most authoritative global expositions of the content of international human rights law, and they set forth in greater detail most of the rights proclaimed in the Universal Declaration.

Of these instruments, the most significant in defining standards related to criminal law and procedure is the Covenant on Civil and Political Rights. Its provisions include references to capital punishment (art. 6), torture and other ill-treatment (art. 7), the right to liberty and freedom from arbitrary detention (art. 9), the rights of detainees (art. 10), the rights of the accused (art. 14), and the prohibition of retroactive penal laws (art. 15).[76] Other provisions set forth, e.g., the rights to freedom of religion, speech, assembly, association, and privacy. In 1984, the UN General Assembly adopted a Convention against Torture, which entered into force in 1987.[77]

The Human Rights Committee, a body of international experts, is responsible for overseeing implementation of the Covenant on Civil and Political Rights. Its functions are exercised in three ways: by comments on the periodic reports on human rights practices which each state party to the Covenant is required to submit, under article 40 of the Covenant; by so-called "general comments" adopted from time to time by the Committee on specific rights or issues; and through the adoption of "views" (which are technically non-binding) on whether or not individual complaints filed under the Optional Protocol disclose violations of the Covenant.[78] The present work relies primarily on the last two mentioned sources for interpretations of the Covenant, although the Committee's jurisprudence thus far is relatively slim and is concerned mainly with gross violations of human rights—murder, torture, "disappearances", detention without trial, etc.—rather than with the intricacies of criminal procedure.[79]

There are numerous other human rights treaties of global application, less relevant for present purposes, which deal with specific issues such as race and sex discrimination, apartheid, slavery, and genocide. In addition,

---

[75]*Adopted* 16 Dec. 1966, *entered into force* 3 Jan. 1976, 999 U.N.T.S. 3 (1966), *reprinted in* R. LILLICH, *supra* note 16, at 180.1.

[76]The texts of these and other relevant provisions may be found in Appendix 2.

[77]Convention against Torture and Other Cruel, Inhuman or Degrading Treatment or Punishment, *adopted* 10 Dec. 1984, *entered into force* 28 June 1987, G.A. Res. 39/46, 39 UN GAOR, Supp. (No. 51) at 197 (1984), *reprinted in* R. LILLICH, *supra* note 16, at 421.1.

[78]*Cf.* Appendix 1. For a discussion of the jurisdiction of the Human Rights Committee and other international oversight bodies, see *infra* at 15–16.

[79]One should recall that the Covenant has been in force for only 13 years. As of 1 Sept. 1988, there were 87 parties to the Covenant, including essentially all of Western Europe, Canada, Australia, and New Zealand; Eastern Europe and the U.S.S.R.; and a geographically and politically diverse number of countries from Latin America, Asia, and Africa. UNITED NATIONS, STATUS OF INTERNATIONAL INSTRUMENTS (1987 & Supp. 1988).

there are now three regional systems for the protection of human rights, in Europe, the Americas, and Africa. While the African Charter on Human and Peoples' Rights[80] entered into force only in 1986, the European and inter-American systems have developed considerable relevant jurisprudence in the area of criminal law and are as important as the UN-based treaties in offering persuasive interpretations of international norms.[81]

All 21 members of the Council of Europe are parties to the European Convention on Human Rights,[82] which entered into force in 1953 and which is overseen by the European Commission and Court of Human Rights. The decisions of these two bodies are generally well-reasoned, legalistic, and textually based on the European Convention in much the same manner as U.S. Supreme Court opinions. Given the shared values and traditions and similar legal systems (at least in the United Kingdom), this body of European jurisprudence developed over the past 35 years offers the most significant and relevant comparisons with substantive U.S. law.

Within the inter-American system, the American Declaration on the Rights and Duties of Man[83] and the American Convention on Human Rights[84] are analogous to the Universal Declaration and the Covenants, respectively; the former was adopted in 1948, while the latter entered into force in 1978. The Inter-American Commission on Human Rights has been an organ of the Organization of American States since the mid-1960s, while the Inter-American Court of Human Rights was created only with the coming into force of the American Convention. As most of the cases with which the Inter-American Commission deals concern gross violations of the right to life, arbitrary detention, and the suppression of political opposition, its decisions tend to rely more on factual findings than on legal analysis; the Court had issued nine Advisory Opinions and delivered a judgment in its first contentious case by the end of 1988.

Also of importance are certain non-treaty international instruments which have acquired persuasive force through their widespread acceptance by the world community. Those with direct relevance to criminal law and procedure and the treatment of prisoners include the UN Stan-

---

[80] *Adopted* 27 June, 1981, *entered into force* 21 Oct. 1986, O.A.U. Doc. CAB/LEG/67/3 Rev.5, *reprinted in* R. LILLICH, *supra* note 16, at 530.1 [hereinafter cited as "African"].

[81] *Cf.* Appendix 1.

[82] *Signed* 4 Nov. 1950, *entered into force* 3 Sept. 1953, 213 U.N.T.S. 222, *reprinted in* R. LILLICH, *supra* note 16, at 500.1 [hereinafter cited as "European"].

[83] *Signed* 2 May 1948, O.A.S. Off. Rec. OEA/Ser.L/V/II.23, doc. 21 rev. 6, *reprinted in* R. LILLICH, *supra* note 16, at 430.1.

[84] *Signed* 22 Nov. 1969, *entered into force* 18 July 1978, O.A.S.T.S. No. 36, at 1, O.A.S. Off. Rec. OEA/Ser.L/V/II.23, doc.21, rev.6, *reprinted in* R. LILLICH, *supra* note 16, at 190.1 [hereinafter cited as "American"].

dard Minimum Rules for the Treatment of Prisoners and other instruments discussed in the section on conditions of detention, *infra* at 63–70.

The United States is a party only to the UN and OAS Charters, three conventions and protocols on slavery, the Protocol Relating to the Status of Refugees, and to minor conventions on the political rights of women. The United States has signed, but not ratified, the Covenant on Civil and Political Rights, American Convention on Human Rights, and Convention against Torture.[85]

Jurisdiction and Powers of International Human Rights Bodies

The interpretations that any tribunal or other body gives to substantive legal provisions may vary, depending on the purpose for which an interpretation is requested and the binding or non-binding nature of the decision rendered. Among the international bodies whose opinions are referred to in the present work, only the European and Inter-American Courts of Human Rights have the authority to issue legally binding judgments, and acceptance of the jurisdiction of both courts is optional.[86]

Even in the context of individual complaints,[87] other international bodies only have the competence to offer technically non-binding opinions as to whether the cases before them constitute violations of the relevant treaties. Thus, the United States is probably under no specific legal obligation to apply the opinion of the Inter-American Commission on Human Rights in the *Roach* case, which held that U.S. law failed to protect the right to life in the context of the execution of those who were juveniles at the time they committed a capital offense.[88] In the great majority of instances, however, countries have complied with the decisions of international bodies such as the European and Inter-American Commissions on Human Rights and the Human Rights Committee.

The European and Inter-American Courts of Human Rights have the

---

[85]*See* R. LILLICH, *supra* note 16, for summaries of U.S. action with respect to these and other treaties.

[86]American, art. 62; European, art. 46. All 21 parties to the European Convention on Human Rights have currently accepted the European Court's jurisdiction; as of the end of 1988, 10 of the parties to the American Convention on Human Rights also had accepted the jurisdiction of the Inter-American Court.

[87]The competence of the Inter-American Commission on Human Rights extends to individual complaints made against any member of the OAS (American, art. 44; Statute of the Commission, art. 20), and the limited competence of the African Commission on Human and Peoples' Rights also is mandatory (African, art. 55). Jurisdiction over individual complaints is optional under art. 25 of the European Convention on Human Rights (although all 21 parties have made the required declaration permitting such complaints) and the Optional Protocol to the Covenant on Civil and Political Rights.

[88]*See* text at and accompanying note 303 *infra*.

power to order that compensation be paid to individuals whose human rights have been violated[89] and that any violations cease, but their judgments do not have automatic domestic effect. Thus, the state concerned is under an obligation to amend or repeal the offending legislation, release a detainee, or pay the ordered compensation, but international courts do not have direct powers of enforcement. It is rare that an international body will order a state to take specific measures which would be equivalent to a domestic order reversing the decision of a lower court or directing executive authorities to take a certain course of action. In general, international judgments (except those which award specific compensation) are analogous to a domestic court's remand of a case for further action consistent with the opinion rendered.

[89]American, art. 63; European, art. 50.

"LIBERTY"

Abuse of powers of arrest and detention is perhaps the most widespread human rights violation in the world. It is the most common form of repression against political opposition groups within a country, and its use is often cloaked in the mantle of "national security" or an equivalent phrase which seeks to excuse the purely political nature of the detention.

The general international standard is that everyone is entitled to "liberty and security of person" and that no one may be subjected to "arbitrary" arrest or detention.[90] While some commentators have suggested that "arbitrary" is merely equivalent to "illegal",[91] the more well-reasoned majority view is that the notion of "arbitrary" includes both procedural and substantive components. A report on arbitrary arrest, detention, and exile by a special committee of the UN Commission on Human Rights concluded:

> [T]he Committee has come to the opinion that "arbitrary" is not synonymous with "illegal" and that the former signifies more than the latter. It seems clear that, while an illegal arrest or detention is almost always arbitrary, an arrest or detention which is in accordance with law may nevertheless be arbitrary. The Committee, therefore, . . . has adopted the following definition: an arrest or detention is arbitrary if it is (a) on grounds or in accordance with procedures other than those established by law, or (b) under the provisions of a law the purpose of which is incompatible with respect for the right to liberty and security of person.[92]

---

[90]UnivDec, arts. 3, 9; CivPol, art. 9; American, art. 7; European, art. 5; African, art. 6.

[91]*See, e.g.*, references contained in UNITED NATIONS, STUDY OF THE RIGHT OF EVERYONE TO BE FREE FROM ARBITRARY ARREST, DETENTION AND EXILE 5–7 (1964); Dinstein, ***The Right to Life, Physical Integrity, and Liberty***, in THE INTERNATIONAL BILL OF RIGHTS, THE COVENANT ON CIVIL AND POLITICAL RIGHTS 130–31 (L. Henkin ed. 1981); M. BOSSUYT, GUIDE TO THE *TRAVAUX PREPARATOIRES* OF THE INTERNATIONAL COVENANT ON CIVIL AND POLITICAL RIGHTS 196–202 (1987).

[92]STUDY ON ARBITRARY ARREST, ***supra*** note 91, at 7.

A similar analysis applies, *mutatis mutandis*, to the concept of "lawful", which includes not only compatibility with procedural due process but also compliance with substantive international human rights norms. The European Court of Human Rights, for example, has stated that the phrase "in accordance with the law" includes the requirements that a norm be accessible, formulated with sufficient precision to enable a citizen reasonably to foresee the consequences a given action may entail, and be itself compatible with the rule of law, i.e., not be open to arbitrary application which would interfere with protected human rights.[93]

At least one U.S. court has held that prohibition against arbitrary arrest and detention is directly binding on the United States as a part of customary international law. In *Fernandez v. Wilkinson*,[94] the court cited, *inter alia*, the Universal Declaration of Human Rights, American Convention on Human Rights, Covenant on Civil and Political Rights, and European Convention on Human Rights, and concluded: "Perpetuating a state of affairs which results in the violation of an alien's fundamental human rights is clearly an abuse of discretion on the part of the responsible agency officials. This Court is bound to declare such an abuse and to order its cessation."[95]

The right to liberty protected by the Fifth and Fourteenth Amendments to the U.S. Constitution has received no authoritative interpretation by U.S. courts, but it is clear that this "broad and majestic term"[96] encompasses more than simply freedom from physical restraint.

> [Liberty] denotes not merely freedom from bodily restraint but also the right of the individual to contract, to engage in any of the common occupations of life, to acquire useful knowledge, to marry, establish a home and bring up children, to worship God according to the dictates of his own conscience and generally to enjoy those privileges long recognized . . . as essential to the orderly pursuit of happiness by free men.[97]

One reason for this expansive definition of "liberty" may be historical,

---

[93]*See* Olsson v. Sweden, App. No. 10465/83, Eur. Court H.R., Judgment of 24 Mar. 1988, Ser. A No. 130, at 25; Sunday Times v. U.K., App. No. 6538/74, *id.*, Judgment of 26 Apr. 1979, Ser. A, No. 30, at 30–31. *Compare* the U.S. void-for-vagueness doctrine, which requires that persons have fair warning of prohibited conduct and that law enforcement officials not be given such wide discretion that arbitrary or discriminatory enforcement could result. *Cf.*, *e.g.*, Kolender v. Lawson, 461 U.S. 352 (1983) (overly broad discretion given to police to require identification); Papachristou v. City of Jacksonville, 405 U.S. 156 (1972) (vagrancy ordinance void as not sufficiently understandable to poor, minorities, or average householder); W. LAFAVE AND A. SCOTT, CRIMINAL LAW 90–97 (2d ed. 1986).

[94]*See* note 42 *supra* and accompanying text.

[95]505 F. Supp. 787, 799.

[96]Board of Regents v. Roth, 408 U.S. 564, 571 (1972).

[97]*Id.* at 569–70, 575.

as the Supreme Court began a process of identifying "fundamental" rights to which the due process clause of the Fourteenth Amendment applied, rather than directly incorporating the guarantees found in the Bill of Rights.[98] Beginning in the 1930s, the court adopted the concept of "selective incorporation," whereby specific provisions of the Bill of Rights were held to be applicable to the states if they were so fundamental as to be "implicit in the concept of ordered liberty."[99] "Liberty" interests which the states had to protect thus came to include a wide selection of rights guaranteed under the guise of "substantive due process".

Individual rights are specifically enumerated under international human rights law in much the same manner as in the U.S. Bill of Rights, and there has been no need to expand the concepts of liberty or due process beyond their obvious connotations of freedom from physical restraint and procedural fairness. Non-physical "liberty" interests are protected internationally through specific guarantees of, e.g., freedom of conscience, expression, religion, and movement and rights to protection for family and private life.[100]

The European Commission of Human Rights, for example, has adopted a narrow interpretation of the term "liberty and security of person" which appears in the European Convention on Human Rights, stating that the provision "must be read as a whole and, in view of its context, as referring only to physical liberty and security. 'Liberty of person' in Article 5(1) thus means freedom from arrest and detention, and 'security of person' the protection against arbitrary interference with this liberty."[101]

While many international treaties, such as the Covenant on Civil and Political Rights and American Convention on Human Rights, merely prohibit "arbitrary" arrest and detention,[102] the European Convention establishes a more explicit standard. The only grounds upon which a person may be "deprived of his liberty" are:

> (a) the lawful detention of a person after conviction by a competent court;
>
> (b) the lawful arrest or detention of a person for non-compliance with the lawful order of a court or in order to secure

---

[98]*Cf., e.g.*, W. LAFAVE & J. ISRAEL, *supra* note 3, at 32–60; J. NOWAK, R. ROTUNDA & J. YOUNG, *supra* note 69, at 452–61.

[99]Palko v. Connecticut, 302 U.S. 319, 325 (1937).

[100]*See generally* H. HANNUM, MATERIALS ON INTERNATIONAL HUMAN RIGHTS AND U.S. CONSTITUTIONAL LAW (1985).

[101]Adler et al. v. F.R.G., Apps. Nos. 5573 & 5670/72, Eur. Comm. H.R., dec. on admissibility of 16 July 1976, 20 Y.B. EUR. CONV. ON HUMAN RIGHTS 102, 7 Dec. & Rep. 8, 26.

[102]CivPol, art. 9; American, art. 7.

the fulfilment of any obligation prescribed by law;

(c) the lawful arrest or detention of a person effected for the purpose of bringing him before the competent legal authority on reasonable suspicion of having committed an offence or when it is reasonably considered necessary to prevent his committing an offence or fleeing after having done so;

(d) the detention of a minor by lawful order for the purpose of educational supervision or his lawful detention for the purpose of bringing him before the competent legal authority;

(e) the lawful detention of persons for the prevention of the spreading of infectious diseases, of persons of unsound mind, alcoholics or drug addicts, or vagrants; [and]

(f) the lawful arrest or detention of a person to prevent his effecting an unauthorized entry into the country or of a person against whom action is being taken with a view to deportation or extradition.[103]

Among the acts considered by the European Commission or Court to constitute "deprivations of liberty" (some of which may be nevertheless justified under the particular exceptions contained in the remainder of the paragraph) are a requirement that vagrants report to the police, even with the former's "voluntary" agreement;[104] the placing of a recidivist "at the Government's disposal" for a ten-year period after completion of a prison sentence;[105] revocation of parole;[106] the confinement of persons to private houses in territory occupied by the armed forces;[107] and taking a person by force to a medical institution for a blood test.[108] Among the situations in which no deprivation of liberty was found are the informal questioning of children in a police station;[109] imposition of disciplinary measures against a convicted prisoner (although such measures may violate the prohibition against inhuman or degrading treatment or punishment);[110] the transfer of a prisoner from one prison hospital to another;[111] detention for

---

[103]European, art. 5(1).

[104]"Vagrancy Cases," *infra* note 202.

[105]Van Droogenbroeck v. Belgium, Eur. Court H.R., Judgment of 24 June 1982, Ser. A No. 50.

[106]*See* discussion *infra* at 125–30.

[107]Cyprus v. Turkey, App. No. 6870/73, Eur. Comm. H.R., Report of 10 July 1976.

[108]X v. Austria, App. No. 8278/78, Eur. Comm. H.R., dec. on admissibility of 13 Dec. 1979, 18 Dec. & Rep. 154.

[109]X v. F.R.G., App. No. 8819/79, Eur. Comm. H.R., dec. on admissibility of 19 Mar. 1981, 24 Dec. & Rep. 158.

[110]X v. Switzerland, App. No. 7754/77, Eur. Comm. H.R., dec. on admissibility of 9 May 1977, 11 Dec. & Rep. 216. *Cf.* discussion *infra* at 59–63.

[111]Ashingdane v. U.K., App. No. 8225/78, Eur. Court H.R., Judgment of 28 May 1985, Ser. A No. 93.

such a short time (a few hours) that no domestic remedies could have been invoked and no actual prejudice was suffered;[112] and imposition of a curfew.[113]

The few European cases which have interpreted "security of person" have excluded, e.g., any requirement that the government provide personal protection to a person who believes that his life is in danger;[114] issues arising in the context of deportation or the application of immigration legislation;[115] and the retention by police of photographs taken at an unlawful public demonstration.[116]

The distinction between deprivation of liberty and restrictions on freedom of movement (the latter is guaranteed under art. 2 of Protocol No. 4 to the European Convention) was addressed by the European Commission and Court of Human Rights in a case involving a compulsory residence order issued under an Italian anti-Mafia law, under which the applicant was required to live in a small area of Asinara, an island which forms part of the island of Sardinia.[117]

> In considering the applicant's actual position during his stay at Cala Reale [the area to which he was confined] the Commission attributes particular importance to the following factors: the area within the limits of which the applicant was confined, the supervision to which he was subjected, the possibilities of social contacts and the period for which the restrictions were imposed.
>
> . . .
>
> [T]he space within which the applicant has to live was much larger than that of a cell. But the concept of deprivation of liberty cannot be identified with detention in a cell. . . . The presence or absence of a physical fence is not a decisive factor. . . . [118]
>
> The Court recalls that in proclaiming the "right to liberty", Article 5(1) is contemplating the physical liberty of the person; its aim is to ensure that no one should be dispossessed of this

---

[112]X and Y v. Sweden, App. No. 7376/76, Eur. Comm. H.R., dec. on admissibility of 7 Oct. 1976, 7 Dec. & Rep. 123.

[113]Cyprus v. Turkey, *supra* note 107.

[114]X v. Ireland, App. No. 6040/73, Eur. Comm. H.R., dec. on admissibility of 20 July 1973, 16 Y.B. EUR. CONV. ON HUMAN RIGHTS 388.

[115]Agee v. U.K., App. No. 7729/76, Eur. Comm. H.R., dec. on admissibility of 17 Dec. 1976, 7 Dec. & Rep. 164; 35 East African Asians v. U.K., App. No. 4626/70, Eur. Comm. H.R., dec. on admissibility of 6 Mar. 1978, 13 Dec. & Rep. 5. But see Bozano v. France, discussed *infra* note 224.

[116]X v. U.K., App. No. 5877/72, Eur. Comm. H.R., dec. on admissibility of 12 Oct. 1973, 16 Y.B. EUR. CONV. ON HUMAN RIGHTS 328.

[117]Guzzardi v. Italy, App. No. 7367/76, Eur. Comm. H.R., Report of 7 Dec. 1978; Eur. Court H.R., Judgment of 6 Nov. 1980, Ser. A No. 39.

[118]Eur. Comm. H.R., *supra* note 117, at paras. 94–95.

liberty in an arbitrary fashion. . . . In order to determine whether someone has been "deprived of his liberty" within the meaning of Article 5, the starting point must be his concrete situation and account must be taken of a whole range of criteria such as the type, duration, effects and manner of implementation of the measure in question.

The difference between deprivation of and restriction upon liberty is nonetheless merely one of degree or intensity, and not one of nature or substance. Although the process of classification into one or other of these categories sometimes proves to be no easy task in that some borderline cases are a matter of pure opinion, the Court cannot avoid making the selection upon which the applicability or inapplicability of Article 5 depends. . . . [At the time the case was decided, Italy had not ratified Protocol No. 4 to the Convention, which deals with restrictions on freedom of movement.]

The Government's reasoning. . . . demonstrates very clearly the extent of the difference between the applicant's treatment on Asinara and classic detention in prison or strict arrest imposed on a serviceman. Deprivation of liberty may, however, take numerous other forms. Their variety is being increased by developments in legal standards and in attitudes; and the Convention is to be interpreted in the light of the notions currently prevailing in democratic States.

Whilst the area around which the applicant could move far exceeded the dimensions of a cell and was not bounded by any physical barrier, it covered no more than a tiny fraction of an island to which access was difficult and about nine-tenths of which was occupied by a prison. . . . Supervision was carried out strictly and on an almost constant basis. Thus, Mr. Guzzardi was not able to leave his dwelling between 10 p.m. and 7 a.m. without giving prior notification to the authorities in due time. He had to report to the authorities twice a day and inform them of the name and number of his correspondent whenever he wished to use the telephone. He needed the consent of the authorities for each of his trips to Sardinia or the mainland, trips which were rare and, understandably, made under the strict supervision of the *carabinieri*. He was liable to punishment by "arrest" if he failed to comply with any of his obligations. Finally, more than sixteen months elapsed between his arrival at Cala Reale and his departure. . . .

It is admittedly not possible to speak of "deprivation of liberty" on the strength of any one of these factors taken individually, but cumulatively and in combination they certainly raise an

> issue of categorisation from the viewpoint of Article 5. . . .
>
> The Court considers on balance that the present case is to be regarded as one involving deprivation of liberty.[119]

Only the European system has dealt with such borderline cases involving restrictions on physical liberty; the Inter-American Commission on Human Rights and Human Rights Committee have been primarily concerned with obvious instances of detention or imprisonment. "Security of person" in the inter-American context has often been employed to refer to the obligation of a government to protect a person from violations of personal integrity, i.e., ensuring the right to life and protection from torture and other physical ill-treatment and preventing so-called "disappearances" of persons taken into custody by the government.

---

[119]Eur. Court H.R., *supra* note 117, at 32–35. Since the residence order was a preventive rather than punitive measure and was not imposed after "conviction by a competent court", the Commission and Court agreed that it violated the Convention.

Arrest and Bail

Suspects' Rights

International standards do not require the full panoply of "Miranda" warnings mandated under the Fifth Amendment,[120] but they do require that anyone arrested "be informed, at the time of arrest, of the reasons for his arrest and shall be promptly informed of any charges against him."[121] Parallel provisions require that a criminal defendant "be informed promptly and in detail in a language which he understands of the nature and cause of the charge against him,"[122] once charges have been filed.

International bodies do not interpret these requirements as technically as U.S. courts, and the standards themselves are much more general than the precise information which must be communicated to suspects under *Miranda*. The European Commission on Human Rights has stated that information relating to the nature of the charge or reason for arrest need not be given in writing,[123] nor need it include a complete description of the possible charges.[124]

> It is the meaning of Article 5(2), that a person should know why he is arrested by the police. The further purpose behind the guarantee . . . is to enable the arrested person to challenge the reasonableness of the suspicion against him because this is a substantive requirement for detaining him under Article 5(1)(c).
> . . .

---

[120] *I.e.*, the right of a suspect to be warned prior to a custodial interrogation of his or her right to remain silent, the fact that any statement made may be used as evidence, and the right to retained or appointed counsel. Miranda v. Arizona, 384 U.S. 436, 444 (1966).

[121] CivPol, art. 9(2). Similar provisions may be found in the American (art. 7(4)) and European (art. 5(2)) conventions, although the required notification must only be given "promptly," rather than specifically at the time of arrest; the latter adds the requirement that the notification be "in a language which he understands."

[122] CivPol, art. 14(3)(a). Essentially identical language is found in art. 8(2)(b) of the American Convention and art. 6(3)(a) of the European Convention.

[123] X v. Netherlands, App. No. 1211/61, Eur. Comm. H.R., dec. on admissibility of 4 Oct. 1962, 9 Coll. Dec. 46.

[124] Neilsen v. Denmark, App. No. 343/57, Eur. Comm. H.R., dec. on admissibility of 2 Sept. 1959, 2 Y.B. Eur. Conv. on Human Rights 412.

> The arrested person should therefore be informed sufficiently about the facts and the evidence which are proposed to be the foundation of a decision to detain him. In particular, he should be enabled to state whether the admits or denies the alleged offense.[125]

In one leading case, a suspect had been previously detained for eleven weeks, interrogated by an investigating judge for several days, and confronted by a witness before being arrested a second time; the Commission found that he "must have been fully aware of the reasons for his arrest and the nature of the charges against him."[126] Informing persons detained for interrogation of the legal basis for their detention (e.g., that they were detained under a particular statute in order to ascertain whether they were involved in or had knowledge of terrorist acts) also has been found to be sufficiently specific to fall within the requirement of article 5(2).[127] Even where the arrest warrant is in a language the accused does not understand, subsequent oral examination by the investigating judge in an appropriate language may be sufficient.[128]

Even under the relatively permissive limits of the European Convention, however, some reasons must be given to a suspect for his or her arrest. Thus, the practice of military police in Northern Ireland of informing only those arrestees who were subsequently charged (but not those released without charge) of the reasons for their arrest violated the European Convention's requirements; mere reference to "emergency powers" was insufficient.[129] Failure to give detailed information to a psychiatric detainee's lawyers, where the detainee could not comprehend the situation, also has been held to violate the Convention.[130]

Judicial Oversight of Arrest and Initial Detention

Anyone arrested or detained on a criminal charge or on suspicion of having committed a crime must be brought "promptly" before a "judge or

---

[125]X v. F.R.G., App. No. 8098/77, Eur. Comm. H.R., dec. on admissibility of 13 Dec. 1978, 16 Dec. & Rep. 111, 113–14. *Compare* Colorado v. Spring, 107 S.Ct. 851 (1987), which held that the fact that a suspect did not know the entire subject matter of an investigation did not invalidate his otherwise voluntary waiver of his privilege against self-incrimination.

[126]Neumeister v. Austria, App. No. 1936/63, Eur. Comm. H.R., dec. on admissibility of 6 July 1964, 14 Coll. Dec. 38, 50.

[127]McVeigh, O'Neill & Evans v. U.K., *infra* note 182.

[128]Delcourt v. Netherlands, App. No. 2689/65, Eur. Comm. H.R., dec. on admissibility of 7 Feb. 1967, 22 Coll. Dec. 48.

[129]Ireland v. U.K., App. No. 5310/71, Eur. Court H.R., Judgment of 18 Jan. 1978, Ser. A No. 25, at 75–77; Eur. Comm. H.R., Report of 25 Jan. 1976, 19 Y.B. EUR. CONV. ON HUMAN RIGHTS 512, 572–74.

[130]X v. U.K., App. No. 6998/75, Eur. Comm. H.R., Report of 16 July 1980 (unpublished), *excerpts reprinted in* COUNCIL OF EUROPE, 1 DIGEST OF STRASBOURG CASE-LAW RELATING TO THE

other officer authorised by law to exercise judicial power."[131] This right is separate from the right to challenge detention before a court, the international equivalent of habeas corpus, which is available to all detainees, not just those detained in connection with criminal charges.[132]

A 1979 decision by the European Court of Human Rights considers this phrase in detail and remains the leading case on the practical obligations of a state under this provision.[133]

> In providing that an arrested person shall be brought promptly before a "judge" or "other officer," Article 5 §3 leaves the Contracting States a choice between two categories of authorities. It is implicit in such a choice that these categories are not identical. However, the Convention mentions them in the same phrase and presupposes that these authorities fulfil similar functions; it thus clearly recognises the existence of a certain analogy between "judge" and "officer." Besides, were this not so, there would scarcely be any explanation for the inclusion of the adjective "other."
>
> "*Magistrat*" in French and, even more, "officer" in English manifestly have a wider meaning than "*juge*" and "judge."
>
> Again, the exercise of "judicial power" is not necessarily confined to adjudicating on legal disputes. In many Contracting States, officers (*magistrats*) and even judges exercise such power without adjudicating, for example members of the prosecuting authorities and investigating judges.
>
> A literal analysis thus suggests that Article 5 §3 includes officials in public prosecutors' departments as well as judges sitting in court (*les magistrats du parquet comme ceux du siège*).
>
> As regards the context of the words falling to be interpreted, the Government and the [European] Commission [of Human Rights] note that throughout Article 5 use is made of expressions of two kinds, one precise—"court" (§1 (a) and (b), §4) and "judge" (§3)—and the other rather vague—"competent legal authority" (§1(c)) and "officer authorised by law to exercise judicial power" (§3). In their view, it is reasonable to deduce from this that the first kind of expression contemplates stricter requirements than the second kind.

EUROPEAN CONVENTION ON HUMAN RIGHTS 379–80 (6 vols. 1984–85) [hereinafter cited as "STRASBOURG DIGEST"].

[131]CivPol, art. 9(3); American, art. 7(5); European, art. 5(3). The American Convention extends this protection to "[a]ny person detained," while the Covenant and European Convention apply only to those detained in connection with criminal charges.

[132]*See* discussion *infra* at 49–57.

[133]Schiesser v. Switzerland, App. No. 7710/76, European Court of Human Rights, Judgment of 4 Dec. 1979, Ser. A No. 34.

The Court shares this opinion but wishes to emphasise the limits of the distinction which it establishes.

Since paragraph 1(c) forms a whole with paragraph 3, "competent legal authority" is a synonym, of abbreviated form, for "judge or other officer authorised by law to exercise judicial power."

In the present case, greater assistance can be gained from a comparison of paragraphs 3 and 4: unlike paragraph 3, paragraph 4 requires the intervention of a "court." Before a body can properly be regarded as a "court," it must, *inter alia*, be independent of the executive and of the parties, but this also holds good for the "officer" mentioned in paragraph 3: while the "judicial power" he is to exercise, unlike the duties set out in paragraph 4, may not take the form of adjudicating on legal disputes (*"un caractère juridictionnel"*), nonetheless judicial power is likewise inconceivable if the person empowered does not enjoy independence. . . .

According to the Government, the purpose of Article 5 §3 is to guarantee the impartiality and objectivity of the person before whom the individual concerned will be brought. In addition, the Government see the appearance before a judge or other officer as calculated to protect everyone against any unjustified arrest and detention.

For the Commission, the object of the provision under consideration is to afford to individuals deprived of their liberty a special guarantee: recourse not to a specific institution, namely a court, but to a procedure of a judicial nature.

The Court views Article 5 as designed to ensure that no one should be arbitrarily dispossessed of his liberty. This overall purpose entails, in the area covered by paragraph 4, the necessity of following a procedure that has a "judicial character" and gives "guarantees appropriate to the kind of deprivation of liberty in question," without which it would be impossible to speak of a "court." The "officer" referred to in paragraph 3 must, for his part, offer guarantees befitting the "judicial" power conferred on him by law.

To sum up, the "officer" is not identical with the "judge" but must nevertheless have some of the latter's attributes, that is to say he must satisfy certain conditions each of which constitutes a guarantee for the person arrested.

The first of such conditions is independence of the executive and of the parties. This does not mean that the "officer" may not be to some extent subordinate to other judges or officers provided that they themselves enjoy similar independence.

In addition, under Article 5 §3, there is both a procedural and a substantive requirement. The procedural requirement places the "officer" under the obligation of hearing himself the individual brought before him; the substantive requirement imposes on him the obligations of reviewing the circumstances militating for or against detention, of deciding, by reference to legal criteria, whether there are reasons to justify detention and of ordering release if there are no such reasons. . . .

[T]he Court emphasises that in the present case the District Attorney intervened exclusively in his capacity as an investigating authority, that is in considering whether Mr. Schiesser should be charged and detained on remand and, subsequently, in conducting enquiries with an obligation to be equally thorough in gathering evidence in his favour and evidence against him. He did not assume the mantle of prosecutor: he neither drew up the indictment nor represented the prosecuting authorities before the trial court. He therefore did not exercise concurrent investigating and prosecuting functions, with the result that the Court is not called upon to determine whether the converse situation would have been in conformity with Article 5 §3. . . .

[T]he Government stress that the Winterthur District Attorney's decision to place Mr. Schiesser in detention on remand was taken in complete independence. . . .

The applicant complains that his lawyer was not allowed to attend the interrogation. . . . but the Court does not consider it to be incompatible with Article 5 §3 of the Convention, which does not make a lawyer's presence obligatory. . . .

The Court is therefore of the opinion that the Winterthur District Attorney offered in the present case the guarantees of independence and the procedural and substantive guarantees inherent in the notion of "officer authorised by law to exercise judicial power."[134]

Despite the dissenting opinions of two judges in *Schiesser*, the European Court and Commission have consistently upheld the appropriateness of utilizing prosecuting attorneys as quasi-judicial officers in bail hearings and for the purpose of determining whether or not an arrestee should continue to be detained pending trial, so long as there is *de facto* separation of the two functions in the particular circumstances. Where a single person exercises both of these functions, however, or has no authority to order a detainee's release, a violation of article 5(3) has been found.[135]

---

[134]*Id.*, paras. 27-31, 34-35, 36, 38; citations and cross-references omitted.

[135]*See, e.g.*, Pauwels v. Belgium, App. No. 10208/82, Eur. Court H.R., Judgment of 26 May 1988, Ser. A No. 135 (even limited dual role of investigating judge and public prosecutor incompat-

The requirement of "promptness" has been considered in several cases, and, while no fixed rule has been established, the European Commission of Human Rights has noted that "a person should not be detained in normal cases for more than four days without being brought before a judicial authority."[136] The European Court of Human Rights has found that intervals of 8 and 12 days between arrest and appearance before a proper authority "are far in excess of the limits laid down by Article 5 para. 3."[137]

In one of its "general comments" on the equivalent provision of the Covenant on Civil and Political Rights, the Human Rights Committee has stated that "delays must not exceed a few days."[138] In considering a complaint under the Optional Protocol to the Covenant, the Committee unsurprisingly found that incommunicado detention for a month violates the "promptness" requirement.[139]

Detention on Remand and Bail

While the Eighth Amendment to the Constitution forbids excessive bail, it does not establish a right to bail per se.[140] In the United States between 1966 and enactment of the Bail Reform Act of 1984, the only concern of the court was supposed to be imposition of the minimum conditions necessary to ensure the accused's appearance in court.

---

ible with required independence); De Jong, Baljet & Van den Brink v. Netherlands, Apps. Nos. 8805/79, 8806/79 & 9242/81, Eur. Court of Human Rights, Judgment of 22 May 1984, Ser. A No. 77 (1984) (military *auditeur-militair* was not sufficiently independent, as he could not order release and also could be called upon subsequently to be prosecuting attorney in the same case); Van der Sluijs, Zuiderveld & Klappe v. Netherlands, Apps. Nos. 9362, 9363 & 9387/81, Eur. Court of Human Rights, Judgment of 22 May 1984, Ser. A No. 78 (same); Duinhof & Duijf v. Netherlands, Apps. Nos. 9626/81 & 9736/82, Eur. Court of Human Rights, Judgment of 22 May 1984, Ser. A No. 79 (same).

[136]Brogan, Coyle, McFadden, and Tracey v. U.K., Apps. Nos. 11209, 11234 & 11266/84 and 11386/85, Eur. Comm. H.R., Report of 14 May 1987, at para. 106. On the facts of the case, which concerned the detention of persons on "reasonable suspicion" of being involved in terrorist offenses, the Commission found that periods of 5 days, 11 hours, and 6 days, 15½ hours, violated the requirement of promptness, while detention for 4 days, 6 hours, and 4 days, 11 hours, was permissible.

[137]Duinhof & Duijf v. Netherlands, *supra* note 135, at para. 41.

[138]Human Rights Committee, General Comment 8(16) (article 9), *Report of the Human Rights Committee*, 37 UN GAOR, Supp. (No. 40) at 95 (1982).

[139]Motta v. Uruguay, Comm. No. 11/1977 [formerly R.2/11], *Report of the Human Rights Committee*, 35 UN GAOR, Supp. (No. 40) at 140 (1980), *reprinted in* Human Rights Committee, *Selected Decisions under the Optional Protocol* 54 (1985).

[140]*See* S. SALTZBURG, AMERICAN CRIMINAL PROCEDURE: CASES AND COMMENTARY 668–70 (2d ed. 1984); W. LAFAVE & J. ISRAEL, *supra* note 3, at 545–47 and Supp. 1987.

On the particular facts of *Carlson v. Landon*, 342 U.S. 524 (1952), a civil case involving the detention of alien communists awaiting deportation, the Supreme Court held that there was no right to bail under the Eighth Amendment. This holding has been challenged by many commentators who have argued that the *Carlson* decision is historically and theoretically inaccurate. *See, e.g.*, Foote, *The Coming Constitutional Crisis in Bail*, 113 U. PA. L. REV. 959 (1964); see also Tribe, *An Ounce of Detention: Preventive Justice in the World of John Marshall*, 56 VA. L. REV. 371, 399–401 (1971).

Prompted by the concern that many bail decisions were taking place without real standards to temper judicial discretion, the Bail Reform Act of 1984 added dangerousness as an acceptable consideration in determining bail.[141] Under the 1984 Act, likelihood of flight and dangerousness has to be proved by clear and convincing evidence, but the Act also identified certain situations where release would not be presumed, including capital cases, cases with a sentence of greater than ten years, repeat offenders, crimes of violence, and certain drug offenses.[142]

The Bail Reform Act of 1984 soon came under attack, primarily on the ground that individuals could be detained in a manner that infringed upon their presumption of innocence.[143] However, in *United States v. Salerno*,[144] the Supreme Court found that pre-trial detention under the Act was a valid regulatory response to a serious problem, not a punitive action. Justice Rehnquist noted that the statute provided for expedited procedural guarantees to meet due process requirements[145] and that the state had a very strong interest in detaining individuals who posed a threat to the community.

Despite the deferential approach to bail and pre-trial detention evidenced in *Salerno*, arrestees still enjoy protection from excessive detention. For example, the Court of Appeals for the Second Circuit has ruled that pre-trial detention for 12 months is unconstitutional.[146]

At the international level, there is essentially a presumption that accused persons should be released pending trial,[147] but, at least under the European human rights regime, there is no substantive right to parole

---

[141]The Bail Reform Act was part of The Comprehensive Crime Control Act of 1984, Pub. L. No. 98–473, 98 Stat. 1976 (1984), codified at 18 U.S.C. §§ 3141–56 (1988 Supp.). For a review of the impact of the 1984 Act, *see* Applebaum, *As Time Goes By: Pretrial Incarceration Under the Bail Reform Act of 1984 and the Speedy Trial Act of 1974*, 8 CARDOZO L.REV. 1055 (1987).

[142]18 U.S.C. § 3142 (1988 Supp.).

[143]The presumptive detention portion of the Bail Reform Act is challenged in Goldkamp, *Danger and Detention: A Second Generation of Bail Reform*, 76 J. CRIM. L. & CRIMINOLOGY 1 (1985), and Alschuler, *Preventive Pretrial Detention and the Failure of Interest-Balancing Approaches to Due Process*, 85 MICH. L. REV. 510 (1986).

[144]107 S.Ct. 2095 (1987).

[145]The 1984 Act provides the arrestee with the right to assistance of counsel, the right to present evidence, and the privilege of cross-examining the government's witnesses. 18 U.S.C. § 3142(f) (1988 Supp.).

[146]U.S. v. Frisone, 795 F.2d 1 (2d Cir. 1986). See discussion *re* trial within a reasonable time, *infra*, at 105–09.

[147]For example, CivPol art. 9(3) provides: "It shall not be the general rule that persons awaiting trial shall be detained in custody . . ."

[148]*See, e.g.*, X v. U.K., App. No. 6760/74, Eur. Comm. H.R., dec. on admissibility of 12 July 1976, *excerpts reprinted in* 1 STRASBOURG DIGEST 277–78. However, a 30-day prohibition against examination by a detained suspect's lawyer of the relevant files of the examining judge and police was held to violate the requirement of a truly adversary process in which a detainee can challenge his detention. See Lamy v. Belgium, App. No. 10444/83, Eur. Comm. H.R., Report of 8 Oct. 1987.

or release on licence.[148] A requirement of "guarantees" to appear for trial also is permissible.[149] The European Court of Human Rights has additionally recognized the dangers of repetition of the offense (or commission of similar offenses)[150] or suppressing evidence,[151] as well as the nature of the offence and the "wickedness" of the accused,[152] as legitimate concerns in a domestic court's determination of whether to order continued pre-trial detention (and, *mutatis mutandis*, imposing lesser conditions if release is ordered).

Nevertheless, the primary justification under article 5(1)(c) of the European Convention for detention on remand is when it is "reasonably considered necessary to prevent [the accused] committing an offence or fleeing after having done so." While the gravity of the offense and potential punishment are factors in determining whether an accused is likely to flee the jurisdiction, they are not the only ones to be considered.

> Other factors, especially those relating to the character of the persons involved, his morals, his home, his occupation, his assets, his family ties and all kinds of links with the country in which he is being prosecuted may either confirm the existence of a danger of flight or make it appear so small that it cannot justify detention pending trial.
>
> It should also be borne in mind that the danger of flight necessarily decreases as the time spent in detention passes by for the probability that the length of detention on remand will be deducted from the period of imprisonment which the person concerned may expect if convicted, is likely to make the prospect seem less awesome to him and reduce his temptation to flee. . . .
>
> [The amount of bail] is designed to ensure not the reparation of loss but rather the presence of the accused at the hearing. Its amount must therefore be assessed principally by reference to him, his assets and his relationship with the persons who are to provide the security; in other words as to the degree of confidence that is possible that the prospect of loss of the security or of action against the guarantors in case of his non-appearance at

---

[149]CivPol, art. 9(3); American, art. 7(5); European, art. 5(3).

[150]*Cf.*, *e.g.*, Stögmüller v. Austria, App. No. 1607/62, Eur. Court of Human Rights, Judgment of 10 Nov. 1969, Ser. A No. 9; Matznetter v. Austria, App. No. 2178/64, Eur. Court of Human Rights, Judgment of 10 Nov. 1969, Ser. A No. 10; Ringeisen v. Austria, App. No. 2614/65, Eur. Court of Human Rights, Judgment of 16 July 1971, Ser. A No. 13; Ventura v. Italy, App. No. 7438/76, Eur. Comm. H.R., Report of 15 Dec. 1980, 23 D & R 5.

[151]*Cf.*, *e.g.*, Wemhoff v. Fed. Rep. Germany, App. No. 2122/64, Eur. Court of Human Rights, Judgment of 27 June 1968, Ser. A No. 7; Ringeisen v. Austria, *supra* note 150; Ventura v. Italy, *supra* note 150.

[152]Matznetter v. Austria, *supra* note 150, para. 9.

the trial will act as a sufficient deterrent to dispel any wish on his part to abscond.[153]

[153]Neumeister v. Austria, App. No. 1936/63, Eur. Court H.R., Judgment of 27 June 1968, Ser. A No. 8, at 39, 40. *See generally* M.-A. Eissen, *Case-law on Article 5 of the Convention for the Protection of Human Rights and Fundamental Freedoms* 23–27 (Eur. Court H.R., Eng. ed. 1986).

DETENTION

The detailed provisions of article 5(1) of the European Convention on Human Rights and the more general prohibitions against "arbitrary" arrest and detention in other international instruments serve essentially the same function, i.e., ensuring that detention is reasonable, determined fairly, and serves a legitimate purpose. The general accord of these international norms with U.S. law and practice is reflected in the fact that only minor differences were noted by President Carter when he submitted the Covenant on Civil and Political Rights and American Convention on Human Rights to the Senate for its advice and consent in 1978,[154] despite the different modes of analyses under which individual rights to physical liberty are protected under the various systems.

Within the European system, detention must be justified by reference to one of the exceptions specified in article 5(1). Perhaps the most obvious permissible grounds are detention after conviction by a competent court [article 5(1)(a)] or, after a lawful arrest, in order to bring a person before "the competent legal authority" based on "reasonable suspicion" of having committed an offence or "when it is reasonably considered necessary" in order to prevent commission of an offense or flight [article 5(1)(c)].

Any person arrested on one of these latter grounds must be brought promptly before a person authorized to exercise judicial power and tried, if charged, within a reasonable time.[155] Reference to preventing commission of an offense "is not adapted to a policy of general prevention directed against an individual or a category of individuals who . . . present a danger on account of their continuing propensity to crime; it does no more than

---

[154]The only reservation recommended by the President with respect to art. 9 of the Covenant on Civil and Political Rights concerned the fact that U.S. law does not require that an offender benefit from any lesser penalty which may be imposed subsequent to commission of an offense, contrary to art. 9(5); an understanding regarding detention pursuant to the order of a "competent judicial authority" was suggested with respect to art. 7(7) of the American Convention. President's Message, *supra* note 20, at xii, xix.

[155]*See infra* at 105–09.

afford the Contracting States a means of preventing a concrete and specific offence."[156]

The requirement that an arrest or detention be "for the purpose of bringing him before the competent legal authority" excludes preventive or administrative detention, as the European Court of Human Rights made clear in its first judgment.[157] Nor may the government rely on detention "after conviction" unless there is, in fact, an offence and a finding of guilt—which must meet the requirements of a fair trial set forth in article 6.[158]

Under the Covenant on Civil and Political Rights, however, preventive detention is permissible so long as it is not arbitrary and is based on grounds and procedures established by law.[159] This would appear to be consistent with the practice in many countries, including that of the United States during World War II.[160] Of course, all the major international instruments permit derogation from normal protections from arbitrary arrest and detention in time of emergency.[161]

Under the European Convention, it also is permissible to detain minors for "educational supervision" [para. 5(1)(d)]; drug addicts, alcoholics, vagrants, and the mentally ill [para. 5(1)(e)];[162] persons who are

---

[156]Eur. Court H.R., Guzzardi v. Italy, *supra* note 117, at para. 102.

[157]Lawless v. Ireland, App. No. 322/57, Eur. Court H.R., Judgment of 1 July 1961, Ser. A No. 1. The language of art. 5(1)(c) is not quite as clear as the Court suggests, however, and one might query whether detention "when it is reasonably considered necessary to prevent his committing an offence" would not be permissible. Of course, any such detention would be subject to the provisions of art. 5(3), under which any person detained under art. 5(1)(c) must be brought promptly before a judge or other officer and is entitled to a trial within a reasonable time.

[158]*See infra* at 79–115.

[159]Human Rights Committee, General Comment 8(16), *supra* note 138.

[160]*See, e.g.*, the Japanese exclusion and detention cases, Hirabayashi v. U.S., 320 U.S. 81 (1943); Korematsu v. U.S., 323 U.S. 214 (1944); and Ex parte Endo, 323 U.S. 283 (1944).

[161]*See* CivPol, art. 5; European, art. 15; OAS, art. 27. *See generally* Lawless v. Ireland, *supra* note 157; Ireland v. U.K., *supra* note 129; Denmark et al. v. Greece, Apps. Nos. 3321/67 et al., Eur. Comm. H.R., Report of 5 Nov. 1969, 12 Y.B. EUR. CONV. ON HUMAN RIGHTS (1969); T. BUERGENTHAL, R. NORRIS & D. SHELTON, PROTECTING HUMAN RIGHTS IN THE AMERICAS (2d ed. 1986) at 217–39; INTERNATIONAL COMMISSION OF JURISTS, STATES OF EMERGENCY, THEIR IMPACT ON HUMAN RIGHTS (1983); P. SIEGHART, THE INTERNATIONAL LAW OF HUMAN RIGHTS 110–18 (1983); *The Individual's Duties to the Community and the Limitations on Human Rights and Freedoms under Article 29 of the Universal Declaration of Human Rights* (E. Daes, Special Rapporteur), UN Doc. E/CN.4/Sub.2/432/Rev.2 (1983); *Study of the implications for human rights of recent developments concerning situations known as states of siege or emergency* (N. Questiaux, Special Rapporteur), UN Doc. E/CN.4/Sub.2/1982/15 (1982); Buergenthal, *To Respect and Ensure: State Obligations and Permissible Derogations*, in Henkin, *supra* note 91, at 80–91; *Derogation from Guarantees laid down in Human Rights Instruments*, in PROTECTION OF HUMAN RIGHTS IN EUROPE: LIMITS AND EFFECTS (I. Maier ed. 1982) at 123–60; *Symposium: Limitation and Derogation Provisions in the International Covenant on Civil and Political Rights*, 7 HUMAN RIGHTS Q. 1 (1985); International Law Association, Committee on the Enforcement of Human Rights Law, *Interim Report of the Committee* (presented to the Seoul Conference, 1986); *id.*, *Second Interim Report of the Committee* (presented to the Warsaw Conference, 1988).

[162]*See infra* note re AIDS; discussion *infra* at 38–42 re mental illness; "Vagrancy Cases," *infra* note 202. Compare the U.S. prohibition against the criminalization of "crimes of status" in, *e.g.*, Robinson v. California, 370 U.S. 660 (1962); Powell v. Texas, 392 U.S. 514 (1968); *cf.* W. LAFAVE & A. SCOTT, *supra* note 93, at 182–84.

being deported or extradited or who are detained in the context of immigration [para. 5(1)(f)]; or "in order to secure the fulfillment of any obligation prescribed by law" [para. 5(1)(b)]. These additional four exceptions to the right to liberty evidently were drafted to reflect European practice, although other international bodies also might find that such matters are not "arbitrary" and therefore would fall within the scope of permissible deprivations of liberty.

"Reasonable" and "Lawfui" Detention

Under international human rights law, national authorities are granted a certain discretion or "margin of appreciation" in determining in what circumstances detention of suspected criminals or others is warranted, reflecting the fact that international tribunals do not function as domestic courts of appeal. However, the European Court of Human Rights has held that domestic judicial review which is limited to considering only whether administrative decisions were illegal, irrational, procedurally improper, or made in bad faith is not sufficient to constitute the oversight required by article 5(4);[163] such domestic review must include a determination of whether there were reasonable grounds for the administrative actions taken.[164]

It is not entirely clear what standard of review is utilized by the Court and Commission in deciding whether or not an act is "lawful" or "reasonable". For example, the Commission has noted that it "has no power to examine whether, in the course of proceedings before [domestic] courts, municipal law was correctly interpreted and applied by the judicial authorities, unless exceptionally they had acted in bad faith in interpreting and applying the law. . . ."[165] A subsequent decision referred to the Commission's task as being "to satisfy itself that the applicant's detention was not the consequence of some arbitrary action by the authorities".[166]

A more recent case suggests a somewhat more comprehensive review. Where the issue was whether or not pre-trial detention had been unduly prolonged, the Commission first found that the period of detention was in accordance with domestic law but went on to note that, "after having examined the file of the case, it is satisfied that there was reasonable suspicion that the applicant had committed the crimes with which he was charged and that there was a danger that he might abscond and commit further offenses. The applicant has submitted no evidence to

---

[163]*See, e.g.*, Weeks v. U.K., *infra* note 560; Ireland v. U.K., *supra* note 129.

[164]Zamir v. U.K., App. No. 9174/80, Eur. Comm. H.R., Report of 11 Oct. 1983.

[165]X v. Netherlands, App. No. 2621/65, Eur. Comm. H.R., dec. on admissibility of 1 April 1966, 9 Y.B. EUR. CONV. ON HUMAN RIGHTS 474, 480.

[166]X v. Austria, App. No. 3001/66, Eur. Comm. H.R., dec. on admissibility of 30 May 1968, 26 Coll. Dec. 55, 58.

show that the courts were not justified in prolonging his detention on remand. This detention was therefore in conformity with Article 5(1)(c) of the Convention."[167] In one of the only cases in which the Commission found that there was not a "sufficiently precise suspicion or belief to satisfy the requirements of Article 5(1)(c)," detention was upheld on other grounds.[168]

In determining "reasonableness" in such situations, "regard must be had to the circumstances of the case as they appeared at the time of the arrest and detention and not as they may appear at some later date."[169]

> This does not, however, mean that the Commission must put itself in the place of the investigating judge and is called upon to assess the evidence in order to make an independent determination as to whether or not at the time of the applicant's arrest there was sufficient proof to give rise to a reasonable suspicion. Its task is rather to review . . . the decisions taken by the domestic authorities and courts in order to determine, on a *prima facie* basis, whether or not these decisions were reasonable and therefore justified.[170]

Obviously, the fact of a subsequent acquittal does not invalidate an initially reasonable suspicion of guilt.[171]

In any event, it is rare that the European Commission or Court will substitute its own judgment with respect to the facts—such as whether a suspicion is reasonable or a person is mentally ill—for that of the domestic authorities which made the initial determination.

Detention of the Mentally Ill

While the European Commission and Court of Human Rights have consistently held that they have the authority to question the substantive grounds for detaining vagrants or the mentally ill, neither has invalidated a detention on the basis of a finding that a detainee was not, in fact, "of

---

[167]X v. Switzerland, App. No. 6993/75, Eur. Comm. H.R., dec. on admissibility of 10 Dec. 1975 (unpublished), *excerpts reprinted in* 1 STRASBOURG DIGEST 379–80.

[168]McVeigh, O'Neill & Evans v. U.K., *infra* note 182.

[169]Nielsen v. Denmark, App. No. 343/57, Eur. Comm. H.R., Report of 15 Mar. 1961 (unpublished), *excerpts reprinted in* 1 STRASBOURG DIGEST 388. One noted scholar and former President of the European Commission of Human Rights has called the determination of whether a period of detention on remand or up to sentencing is reasonable "a task intricate and difficult." J. FAWCETT, THE APPLICATION OF THE EUROPEAN CONVENTION ON HUMAN RIGHTS 107 (2d ed. 1987). On the issue of the various time periods utilized by the Commission in considering the "reasonable time" aspects of arts. 5 and 6, see *id.* at 105–16.

[170]X v. F.R.G., App. No. 7033/75, Eur. Comm. H.R., dec. on admissibility of 12 Oct. 1977 (unpublished), *excerpts reprinted in* 1 STRASBOURG DIGEST 393–94.

[171]X v. Netherlands, App. No. 7042/75, Eur. Comm. H.R., dec. on admissibility of 7 Mar. 1977 (unpublished), *excerpts reprinted in* 1 STRASBOURG DIGEST 391–93.

unsound mind."[172] However, the Commission and Court split as to whether parental consent was sufficient to justify commitment of an apparently normal 12-year-old child to a psychiatric hospital.[173]

> The Convention does not define the term "person of unsound mind". . . .
>
> However, in providing for the lawful detention of a person of unsound mind, Article 5(1)(e) cannot be regarded as enabling any person whose public or private behaviour deviates from the prevailing standards, ideas or even fashions, to be deprived of his freedom or as allowing States to class as being of unsound mind any citizen considered "asocial" or "marginal."
>
> This is plain from the provision's context as well as from the object and aim of the Convention as a whole. By proclaiming everyone's right to liberty and security of person, Article 5(1) protects the individual from any kind of arbitrary detention. The list of permitted exceptions to this general principle is an exhaustive one. Moreover, according to the general principles of law common to the member States of the Council of Europe, legislation that permits any interference with individual liberty must be strictly interpreted.[174]
>
> The very nature of what has to be established before the competent national authority—that is, a true mental disorder—calls for objective medical expertise. Further the mental disorder must be of a kind or degree warranting compulsory confinement. What is more, the validity of continued confinement depends upon the persistence of such a disorder. . . .[175]

While there is no right under article 5(1)(e) to particular treatment

---

[172]On one occasion, the Court did reject an argument by the Italian government that the preventive detention of a suspected member of the Mafia could be justified on the grounds that he was a vagrant. Guzzardi v. Italy, Eur. Court H.R., *supra* note 117.

[173]*Compare* Neilsen v. Denmark, App. No. 10929/84, Eur. Comm. H.R., Report of 12 Mar. 1987 (art. 5 is relevant to child's detention, which must be capable of being challenged before a court) *with id.*, Eur. Court H.R., Judgment of 28 Nov. 1988, Ser. A No. 144 (parent's request for hospitalization sufficient; no art. 5 liberty interest involved). The Court's decision was reached by a vote of 9 to 7.

[174]Winterwerp v. Netherlands, App. No. 6301/73, Eur. Comm. H.R., Report of 15 Dec. 1977, at paras. 73–75.

[175]Winterwerp v. Netherlands, Eur. Court H.R., *infra* note 177, at para. 39. Also see Ashingdane v. U.K., *supra* note 111; Luberti v. Italy, App. No. 9019/80, Eur. Court H.R., Judgment of 23 Feb. 1984, Ser. A No. 75. *Compare* the U.S. standard that involuntarily commitment to a mental institution must be based on a fair procedure which has determined that the person is dangerous to himself or others. *See, e.g.*, Jones v. U.S., 463 U.S. 354 (1983) (upholding automatic committal following criminal acquittal by reason of insanity); Addington v. Texas, 441 U.S. 418 (1979) (requiring a "clear and convincing" evidence standard for involuntary civil committal); O'Connor v. Donaldson, 422 U.S. 563 (1975).

appropriate to a mental patient's condition,[176] persons detained as mentally ill have the right to challenge the lawfulness of their detention before a court, initially and at regular intervals thereafter. The leading case on this issue is *Winterwerp v. Netherlands*,[177] in which a person was initially detained for six weeks under an emergency procedure by the local burgomaster and subsequently held under a judicial detention order (made on his wife's application) renewed annually upon the request of the public prosecutor and on the basis of medical reports from the detainee's doctor. After determining that Winterwerp's initial detention was proper, the Court turned to the issue of whether his continuing detention was compatible with the European Convention.

> [T]he reasons initially warranting confinement of this kind [i.e., on grounds of mental disorder] may cease to exist. Consequently, it would be contrary to the object and purpose of Article 5 to interpret paragraph 4 thereof, read in its context, as making this category of confinement immune from subsequent review of lawfulness merely provided that the initial decision issued from a court. The very nature of the deprivation of liberty under consideration would appear to require a review of lawfulness to be available at reasonable intervals. . . .
>
> The judicial proceedings referred to in Article 5 §4 need not, it is true, always be attended by the same guarantees as those required under Article 6 §1 [regarding the requirements for a "fair trial"] for civil or criminal litigation. Nonetheless, it is essential that the person concerned should have access to a court and the opportunity to be heard either in person or, where necessary, through some form of representation, failing which he will not have been afforded "the fundamental guarantees of procedure applied in matters of deprivation of liberty". Mental illness may entail restricting or modifying the manner of exercise of such a right, but it cannot justify impairing the very essence of the right. Indeed, special procedural safeguards may prove called for in order to protect the interests of persons who, on account of their mental disabilities, are not fully capable of acting for themselves. . . .
>
> As to the particular facts, the applicant was never associated, either personally or through a representative, in the proceedings leading to the various detention orders made against

---

[176]Winterwerp v. Austria, *infra* note 177, at para. 51. For a discussion of a possible "right to treatment" in the U.S., see W. LAFAVE & J. SCOTT, *supra* note 93, at 363–65, and cases cited therein.

[177]App. No. 6301/73, Eur. Court H.R., Judgment of 24 Oct. 1979, Ser. A No. 33.

him: he was never notified of the proceedings or of the outcome; neither was he heard by the courts or given the opportunity to argue his case.

In this fundamental respect, the guarantees demanded by Article 5 §4 of the Convention were lacking both in law and in practice. . . .

While [the relevant Dutch legislation] allows the person concerned to seek a review of his detention, his request for discharge is not necessarily decided on by a court. The request has to be addressed to the hospital authorities who transmit it, if they have received an unfavourable medical opinion, to the public prosecutor. The public prosecutor will in principle then refer the request to the Regional Court, but in certain cases he is not obliged to do so, in particular where it appears manifestly impossible to grant the request. . . .

Mr. Winterwerp was accordingly the victim of a breach of Article 5 §4.

In the light of this conclusion, the Court does not deem it necessary to settle an issue raised in this case, namely whether the review of "lawfulness" provided for by Article 5 §4 covers not only the formal propriety of the procedure followed but also the substantive justification of the deprivation of liberty.[178]

In a subsequent case, the Court addressed the issue left undetermined in *Winterwerp* and also clarified that a person detained on the grounds of mental illness has the right either to automatic periodic review of the detention or to initiate proceedings challenging the detention at reasonable intervals.

[In the present case,] X was transferred from the authority of the courts to the authority of the Home Secretary and committed to a psychiatric hospital for an indefinite period. After releasing him in May 1971, the Home Secretary ordered his return to hospital in April 1974. This was an administrative decision based, in part, on circumstances distinct from those prompting the initial court orders. Furthermore, although the conditions specified under [relevant domestic legislation] depend upon matters, notably medical, which of their nature may change with the passage of time, there was no system of periodic judicial review to verify that these conditions remained satisfied throughout the contested detention. . . .

[A] person of unsound mind compulsorily confined in a psychiatric institution for an indefinite or lengthy period is . . . in

[178] *Id.* at paras. 55–68; citations and cross-references omitted.

principle entitled, at any rate where there is no automatic periodic review of a judicial character, to take proceedings at reasonable intervals before a court to put in issue the "lawfulness". . . of his detention, whether that detention was ordered by a civil or criminal court or by some other authority.

It is not within the province of the Court to inquire into what would be the best or most appropriate system of judicial review in this sphere, for the Contracting States are free to choose different methods of performing their obligations. . . .

[T]he remedy of habeas corpus. . . . may be regarded as adequate . . . for emergency measures for the detention of persons on the ground of unsoundness of mind. Such measures, provided they are of short duration, are capable of being "lawful" under Article 5(1)(e) even though not attended by the usual guarantees such as thorough medical examination. The authority empowered to order emergency detention of this kind must, in the nature of things, enjoy a wide discretion, and this inevitably means that [the] role of the courts will be reduced.

On the other hand, in the Court's opinion, a judicial review as limited as that available in the habeas corpus procedure in the present case is not sufficient for a continuing confinement such as the one undergone by X. Article 5(4), the Government are quite correct to affirm, does not embody a right to judicial control of such scope as to empower the court, on all aspects of the case, to substitute its own discretion for that of the decision-making authority. The review should, however, be wide enough to bear on those conditions which, according to the Convention, are essential for the "lawful" detention of a person on the ground of unsoundness of mind, especially as the reasons capable of initially justifying such a detention may cease to exist. This means that . . . [there must be] an appropriate procedure allowing a court to examine whether the patient's disorder still persisted and whether the Home Secretary was entitled to think that a continuation of the compulsory confinement was necessary in the interests of public safety. . . .[179]

---

[179] X v. U.K., App. No. 6998/75, Eur. Court H.R., Judgment of 5 Nov. 1981, Ser. A No. 46, at paras. 48–54, 58–59. *Also see* C., Medway & Ball v. U.K., Apps. Nos. 7099/75, 7699/76 & 9292/81, Eur. Comm. H.R., Report of 13 July 1983. Judicial oversight does not, however, extend to the kind of treatment or conditions to which a person detained because of mental illness is subjected, although "there must be some relationship between the ground of permitted deprivation of liberty relied on and the place and conditions of detention." Ashingdane v. U.K., *supra* note 111, at para. 44.

Detention to Secure the Fulfillment of a Legal Obligation

The possibility under article 5(1)(b) of detaining a person "in order to secure the fulfillment of an obligation prescribed by law" may at first glance seem "extremely troublesome,"[180] but its use has been limited to compelling a person "to fulfil a specific and concrete obligation which he has until then failed to satisfy. A wide interpretation would entail consequences incompatible with the notion of the rule of law from which the whole Convention draws its inspiration. It would justify, for example, administrative internment meant to compel a citizen to discharge, in relation to any point whatever, his general duty of obedience to the law."[181] Detention would undoubtedly be justified to enforce a specific court order, e.g., through contempt proceedings.

In only one instance has the Commission or Court found detention on this ground to be justified, in the context of a security check by British authorities on persons arriving from Northern Ireland or Ireland.[182] While the decision may have turned on the particular sympathy European bodies have shown for measures designed to suppress terrorism, it does come close to justifying what a dissenting opinion labeled a "fishing expedition" in the absence of any reasonable suspicion.[183]

> [T]he measures at issue here were taken under legislation which was enacted, and has been applied, for the purpose of combatting a campaign of terrorism. This legislation admittedly involves temporary and abnormal restrictions within the field of Convention rights. . . . Nonetheless, the Government have not sought to invoke Art. 15 [permitting derogations from the Convention in time of emergency]. . . .
>
> It is well established in the case-law of the Court that the Convention must be interpreted and applied in the light of present day conditions. The existence of organised terrorism is a feature of modern life whose emergence since the Convention was drafted cannot be ignored any more than the changes in social conditions and moral opinion which have taken place in the same period. It faces democratic Governments with a problem of serious organised crime which they must cope with in order to preserve the fundamental rights of their citizens. The measures they take must comply with the Convention and the Convention

---

[180] Stoiber, *The Right to Liberty: A Comparison of the European Convention on Human Rights with the United States Practice*, 5 HUMAN RIGHTS 333, 339 (1976).

[181] Engel et al. v. Netherlands, *infra* note 490, at para. 69. *Cf.* Ireland v. U.K., *supra* note 129; Lawless v. Ireland, *supra* note 157.

[182] McVeigh, O'Neill & Evans v. U.K., Apps. Nos. 8022, 8025 & 8027/77, Eur. Comm. H.R., Report of 18 Mar. 1981, 25 Dec. & Rep. 5.

[183] *Id.*, slip op. at 71 (diss. op. Mr. Trechsel).

organs must always be alert to the danger in this sphere adverted to by the Court, of "undermining or even destroying democracy on the ground of defending it." However . . . some compromise between the requirements for defending democratic society and individual rights is inherent in the system of the Convention. Particularly in assessing such matters as the "necessity" for a given measure in a "democratic society," specific requirements of the situation facing the society in question must be taken into account. . . .

[In the present case, each of the applicants was detained for a period of 45 hours upon his arrival in Liverpool from Ireland, under the authority of an "examining officer" at the border.] The purpose of such examination . . . is in broad terms to determine (a) whether the person examined appears to be concerned in terrorism, (b) whether he is subject to an exclusion order [from Great Britain] or (c) whether there are grounds for suspecting that he has committed an offence. . . . [relating] to non-compliance with exclusion orders and failure to disclose information concerning terrorism.

It is not necessary, as a matter of domestic law, that the examining officer should suspect or believe that a person has been concerned in terrorism, or is subject to an exclusion order or has committed an offence before he can lawfully effect an arrest [under the applicable legislation]. . . .

The applicants submit . . . that the obligation [which would justify detention under para. 5(1)(b)] . . . must be an antecedent one and some voluntary failure to comply with it must already have taken place before detention to secure its fulfilment is justified. The Commission considers that there is much force in this argument. . . .

Nonetheless, the wording of Art. 5(1)(b) does not expressly require that there should have been such deliberate or negligent failure on the part of the detainee. It requires only that the *purpose* of the detention should be to secure the fulfilment of the obligation. This does not expressly exclude the possibility of detention in the absence of a prior breach of legal duty. However in the Commission's opinion the mere combination of an unfulfilled obligation (even if "specific and concrete"), coupled with the relevant purpose, is not enough for the purposes of Art. 5(1)(b). To hold that it was would open up a clear possibility of arbitrary detention, thus ignoring the object and purpose of Art. 5(1) and the importance of the right to liberty in a democratic society.

In the Commission's opinion there must accordingly be specific circumstances such as to warrant the use of detention as a means of securing the fulfilment of an obligation before detention on this ground can be justified under Art. 5(1)(b). . . . [T]he person concerned must normally have had a prior opportunity to fulfil the "specific and concrete" obligation incumbent on him and have failed, without proper excuse, to do so before it can be said in good faith that his detention is "in order to secure the fulfilment" of the obligation. However, there may . . . be other limited circumstances of a pressing nature which could warrant detention in order to secure fulfilment of an obligation.

Finally, . . . the nature of the obligation whose fulfilment is sought must itself be compatible with the Convention. The obligation in question cannot, in particular, consist in substance merely of an obligation to submit to detention. . . .

The Commission finds that the purpose of the detention "pending . . . examination" of the present applicants was essentially to secure their compliance with the overall obligation to submit to examination. . . . The purpose of their arrest was not therefore to compel them to rectify any specific prior breach of legal duty. . . .

The obligation to submit to examination . . . was not a general obligation arising under criminal or disciplinary law. . . . It arose only in circumstances specified by law, in this case on the applicants' entry into Great Britain, and on the requirement of an examining officer. It can to some extent be seen as comparable in character to other obligations to furnish information in specific circumstances, such as obligations to produce evidence of identity, to make customs declarations or tax returns, or the obligation to furnish an affidavit. . . .

The obligation to submit to examination does not amount to a general obligation to submit to questioning or interrogation on any occasion, or for any purpose. . . . It is in essence an obligation to submit to a security check (if so required) on entering or leaving Great Britain. The purpose of the check is limited to determining the matters set out in [the applicable legislation]. . . .

In all the circumstances, the Commission considers that the obligation imposed on the present applicants to submit to examination was a specific and concrete obligation and that the United Kingdom authorities were therefore *in principle* entitled under Art. 5(1)(b) to resort to detention to secure its fulfilment. In reaching this conclusion the Commission has particularly taken into account the fact that the obligation in question arises only in limited circumstances, namely in the context of passage over a clear geographical or political boundary. Furthermore the purpose of the examination is limited and directed towards an end of evident public importance in the context of a serious and continuing threat from organised terrorism. . . .

[There is] no indication that the detention of the present applicants was arbitrary or effected for any improper purpose. . . . In the exceptional context of the case [the Commission] concludes [by a vote of 13 to 1] that there were thus sufficient circumstances to warrant their arrest and detention for some 45 hours for the purpose of securing fulfilment of the obligation incumbent on them to submit to examination.[184]

Other Justifications for Detention

Neither the Court nor Commission has considered cases which raise issues of the detention of persons with infectious diseases, alcoholics, or drug addicts; the Commission's only case involving a minor upheld detention in an "observation centre" for eight months while police investigated a theft in which he was allegedly involved, on the grounds that the detention was "for the purpose of bringing him before the competent legal authority" under article 5(1)(d).[185]

The broad discretion granted to national authorities with respect to the mentally ill also has been extended to the detention of persons "against whom action is being taken with a view to deportation or

[184] *Id.* at paras. 155-95; emphasis in original; citations and cross-references omitted. The Commission also determined that searching, questioning, fingerprinting, and photographing the applicants and retaining the subsequent records were justified "in the interests of public safety and for the prevention of crime" under art. 8 of the Convention, although there was no reasonable suspicion to connect the applicants with any crime. The Commission ultimately found that there was an unjustifiable interference with the right of two of the applicants to private and family life and correspondence under art. 8, in that the authorities refused to let them communicate with their wives during the duration of their detention. *Compare* U.S. v. Montoya de Hernandez, 473 U.S. 531 (1985), which justified detention of a traveler at the border in order to wait for a bowel movement, if customs agents "reasonably suspect that the traveler is smuggling contraband in her alimentary canal."

[185] X v. Switzerland, App. No. 8500/79, Eur. Comm. H.R., dec. on admissibility of 14 Dec. 1979, 18 Dec. & Rep. 238. *Compare* Schall v. Martin, 467 U.S. 253 (1984), in which the U.S. Supreme Court upheld a New York practice of detaining juveniles before trial, on the grounds that the detention was a regulatory practice, not punishment, and that the detailed procedural protections available satisifed due process.

Query what limitations, perhaps of proportionality, might be placed on the detention of AIDS victims, given the specific exception for preventing "the spreading of infectious diseases" referred to in art. 5(1)(e) of the European Convention?

[186] *See, e.g.*, Agee v. U.K., App. No. 7729/76, Eur. Comm. H.R. dec. on admissibility of 17 Dec. 1976, 7 Dec. & Rep. 164; Caprino v. U.K., App. No. 6871/75, Eur. Comm. H.R., Report of 17 July 1980, 22 Dec. & Rep. 5. The only case in which a violation of the Convention seems to have been found in relation to such proceedings is Bozano v. France, *infra* note 224, in which the abduction of a person and his transfer to Swiss authorities in order to circumvent an adverse ruling by a French court was held to be "unlawful" and a violation of "security of person".

extradition" [art. 5(1)(f)]. As there is no right under the European Convention not to be extradited, deported, or expelled from a country, review by the Commission and Court has been limited to the question of whether an applicant was, in fact, detained in connection with deportation or extradition proceedings, rather than examining the legality of the deportation or extradition order itself.[186] Nor does the limitation of detention to a "reasonable" time in article 5(3) apply to detention under article 5(1)(f), although the Commission has suggested that such detention could be excessive and therefore unlawful if the proceedings which justified the detention were not conducted with "requisite diligence".[187]

[187]*See, e.g.*, Lynas v. Switzerland, App. No. 7317/75, Eur. Comm. H.R., dec. on admissibility of 6 Oct. 1976, 20 Y.B. EUR. CONV. ON HUMAN RIGHTS 412. Detention of up to 10 months (where delay was partly caused by the detainee's own conduct and the matter was complex) has been considered lawful. X v. U.K., App. No. 8081/70, Eur. Comm. H.R., dec. on admissibility of 12 Dec. 1977, 12 Dec. & Rep. 207.

HABEAS CORPUS

The right of every person to have the judiciary determine the legality of his or her detention through the writ of habeas corpus dates from adoption of the English Magna Carta in 1215 and is a fundamental tenet of U.S. criminal law enshrined in the Constitution.[188] The first post-1945 international human rights text[189] provides that "[e]very individual who has been deprived of his liberty has the right to have the legality of his detention ascertained without delay by a court," and other international instruments include comparable provisions.

Under international standards, the initial review of detention (roughly equivalent to arraignment) may be conducted by a court or "other officer authorized by law" to perform this function.[190] However, everyone has an additional right, equivalent to habeas corpus and included within the Latin American concept of *amparo*, "to take proceedings before a court, in order that that court may decide without delay on the lawfulness of his detention and order his release if the detention is not lawful."[191]

In the United States, habeas corpus is generally restricted to the post-trial context, with the "speedy trial" guarantees of the Sixth and Fourteenth Amendments available to seek relief from pre-trial detention.[192] Unlike the situation in the United States, the international equivalent of habeas corpus is not generally available as a means of collaterally attacking unconstitutional or otherwise defective laws, but is restricted to a determination of the initial legality and reasonableness of detention and,

---

[188]U.S. Const., Art. I, § 9, cl. 2: "The Privilege of the Writ of Habeas Corpus shall not be suspended, unless when in Cases of Rebellion or Invasion the public Safety may require it."

[189]American Declaration of the Rights and Duties of Man, *supra* note 83, art. 25.

[190]*See* discussion *supra* at 40–45.

[191]CivPol, art. 9(4). Similar provisions are found in American, art. 7(5); European, art. 5(4). An earlier draft of the Covenant included a reference to a remedy "in the nature of habeas corpus," but this phrase was deleted in order to allow greater flexibility to states. See *Annotations of the text on the draft International Covenants on Human Rights*, UN Doc. A/2929 (1955), chap. VI, para. 35, *quoted in* M. BOSSUYT, *supra* note 91, at 213.

[192]*See, e.g.*, Johnson v. Hoy, 227 U.S. 245 (1913).

in some circumstances, the continuing validity of detention when it is based on factors which may change over time, such as mental illness.

The right of judicial review of detention is commonly among those limited in time of war or other emergency, on grounds of "national security," and the right of habeas corpus is not specifically included among those rights from which no derogation is possible under the three major multilateral conventions which recognize it.[193] Without entering into a discussion of the complex issue of states of emergency, a public emergency recognized under international law must, in general, be imminent, officially proclaimed, and threaten the life or security of the nation.[194] In addition, only those measures "strictly required by the exigencies of the situation" may be taken in derogation from otherwise applicable human rights norms.[195]

The American Convention on Human Rights does prohibit derogation from "the judicial guarantees essential for the protection of such [nonderogable] rights."[196] When asked to interpret this provision, the Inter-American Court of Human Rights held in 1987 that habeas corpus could *not* be suspended in time of emergency, even though it is not specifically designated as nonderogable by the American Convention on Human Rights.

> It cannot be denied that under certain circumstances the suspension of guarantees may be the only way to deal with emergency situations and, thereby, to preserve the highest values of a democratic society. The Court cannot, however, ignore the fact that abuses may result from the application of emergency measures not objectively justified in the light of the requirements prescribed in Article 27 [concerning the suspension of guarantees during emergencies] and the principles contained in other here relevant international instruments. . . . [T]he Court must emphasize that the suspension of guarantees cannot be disassociated from the "effective exercise of representative democracy" referred to in Article 3 of the OAS [Organization of American States] Charter. . . . The suspension of guarantees lacks all legitimacy whenever it is resorted to for the purpose of undermining the democratic system. . . .
>
> The lawfulness of the measures taken to deal with each of

---

[193]*See* CivPol, art. 4; American, art. 27; Europe, art. 15. *Compare* U.S. Const, *supra* note 188. Approximately two-thirds of the declarations filed under art. 4 of the Covenant on Civil and Political Rights include art. 9, in which the right to habeas corpus is guaranteed, among those rights from which derogation is being made. HUMAN RIGHTS: STATUS OF INTERNATIONAL INSTRUMENTS, *supra* note 79, at 58–85.

[194]*See* sources cited *supra* note 161.

[195]*See* CivPol, art. 4; American, art. 27; European, art. 15.

[196]American, art. 27(2).

the special situations referred to in Article 27(1) ["war, public danger, or other emergency that threatens the independence or security of a State Party"] will depend, moreover, upon the character, intensity, pervasiveness, and particular context of the emergency and upon the corresponding proportionality and reasonableness of the measures. . . .

When guarantees are suspended, some legal restraints applicable to the acts of public authorities may differ from those in effect under normal conditions. These restraints may not be considered to be non-existent, however, nor can the government be deemed thereby to have acquired absolute powers that go beyond the circumstances justifying the grant of such exceptional legal measures. . . .

The determination as to what judicial remedies are "essential" for the protection of the rights which may not be suspended will differ depending upon the rights that are at stake. The "essential" judicial guarantees necessary to guarantee the rights that deal with the physical integrity of the human person must of necessity differ from those that seek to protect the right to a name, for example, which is also non-derogable. . . .

The guarantees must be not only essential but also judicial. The expression "judicial" can only refer to those judicial remedies that are truly capable of protecting these rights. Implicit in this conception is the active involvement of an independent and impartial judicial body having the power to pass on the lawfulness of measures adopted in a state of emergency. . . .

[Article 25(1) of the American Convention] is a general provision that gives expression to the procedural institution known as "amparo," which is a simple and prompt remedy designed for the protection of all of the rights recognized by the constitutions and laws of the States Parties and by the Convention. Since "amparo" can be applied to all rights, it is clear that it can also be applied to those that are expressly mentioned in Article 27(2) as rights that are non-derogable in emergency situations.

In its classical form, the writ of habeas corpus, as it is incorporated in various legal systems of the Americas, is a judicial remedy designed to protect personal freedom or physical integrity against arbitrary detention by means of a judicial decree ordering the appropriate authorities to bring the detained person before a judge so that the lawfulness of the detention may be determined and, if appropriate, the release of the detainee be ordered. The Convention proclaims this remedy in Article 7(6). . . .

> [H]abeas corpus performs a vital role in ensuring that a person's life and physical integrity are respected, in preventing his disappearance or the keeping of his whereabouts secret and in protecting him against torture or other cruel, inhumane, or degrading punishment or treatment.
>
> This conclusion is buttressed by the realities that have been the experience of some of the peoples of this hemisphere in recent decades, particularly disappearances, torture and murder committed or tolerated by some governments. This experience has demonstrated over and over again that the right to life and to humane treatment are threatened whenever the right to habeas corpus is partially or wholly suspended. . . .
>
> [I]n a system governed by the rule of law it is entirely in order for an autonomous and independent judicial order to exercise control over the lawfulness of such [emergency] measures by verifying, for example, whether a detention based on the suspension of personal freedom complies with the legislation authorized by the state of emergency. In this context, habeas corpus acquires a new dimension of fundamental importance. . . .
>
> [I]t follows that writs of habeas corpus and of "amparo" are among those judicial remedies that are essential for the protection of various rights whose derogation is prohibited by Article 27(2) and that serve, moveover, to preserve legality in a democratic society. . . .
>
> Therefore. . . . the legal remedies guaranteed in Articles 7(6) and 25(1) of the [American] Convention may not be suspended because they are judicial guarantees essential for the protection of the rights and freedoms whose suspension Article 27(2) prohibits.[197]

In a series of applications which raised similar issues concerning Uruguay, the Human Rights Committee essentially held that denial of the remedy of habeas corpus to persons arrested and detained under "prompt security measures" on grounds that they represented "a grave and imminent danger to security and public order" was a prima facie violation of article 9(4) of the Covenant on Civil and Political Rights.[198] However, the

---

[197]I/A Court H.R., Habeas Corpus in Emergency Situations (Arts. 27(2), 25(1) and 7(6) American Convention on Human Rights), Advisory Opinion OC-8/87 of 30 Jan. 1987, Ser. A No. 8, at 38–48. *Cf.* I/A Court H.R., Judicial Guarantees in States of Emergency (Arts. 27(2), 25 and 8 American Convention on Human Rights), Advisory Opinion OC-9/87 of 6 Oct. 1987, Ser. A No. 9; INTER-AMERICAN COMMISSION ON HUMAN RIGHTS, TEN YEARS OF ACTIVITIES 1971–1981 (1982) at 325–27.

[198]*See, e.g.*, Santullo Valcada v. Uruguay, Comm. No. 9/1977, *Report of the Human Rights Committee*, 35 UN GAOR, Supp. (No. 40) at 113 (1980); Garcia Lanza de Netto et al. v. Uruguay, Comm. No. 8/1977, *id.* at 118; Grille Motta v. Uruguay, Comm. No. 11/1977, *id.* at 140.

Committee's analysis is fairly cursory, due to the failure of Uruguay to contest the complaints in all but the most conclusory fashion.

The international right to have the legality of one's detention judged by a court applies to all forms of detention, not just to imprisonment related to alleged criminal activity. The European Court and Commission of Human Rights, for example, have held article 5(4) of the European Convention applicable with respect to the detention of persons of unsound mind,[199] members of the armed forces,[200] and vagrants.[201]

The European Court of Human Rights has considered the nature of the "court" to which access must be given in a number of cases, most notably in the 1971 "Vagrancy Cases" brought against Belgium.[202]

> [I]t is clear that the purpose of Article 5(4) is to assure to persons who are arrested and detained the right to a judicial supervision of the lawfulness of the measure to which they are thereby subjected. The word "court" ("*tribunal*") is there found in the singular and not in the plural. Where the decision depriving a person of his liberty is one taken by an administrative body, there is no doubt that Article 5(4) obliges the Contracting States to make available to the person detained a right of recourse to a court; but there is nothing to indicate that the same applies when the decision is made by a court at the close of judicial proceedings. In the latter case the supervision required by Article 5(4) is incorporated in the decision; this is so, for example, where a sentence of imprisonment is pronounced after "conviction by a competent court" (Article 5(1)(a) of the Convention). It may therefore be concluded that Article 5(4) is observed if the arrest or detention of a vagrant, provided for in para. (1)(e), is ordered by a "court" within the meaning of para. (4). . . .
>
> [I]n order to constitute such a "court" an authority must provide the fundamental guarantees of procedure applied in matters of deprivation of liberty. If the procedure of the competent authority does not provide them, the State could not be dispensed from making available to the person concerned a second authority which does provide all the guarantees of judicial procedure.

---

[199]Winterwerp v. Netherlands, *supra* note 177.

[200]Engel et al. v. Netherlands, *infra* note 490.

[201]"Vagrancy Cases," *infra* note 202.

[202]De Wilde, Ooms & Versyp v. Belgium ("Vagrancy Cases"), Apps Nos. 2832/66 et al., Eur. Court H.R., Judgment of 18 June 1971, Ser. A No. 12, *summarized in* Cohn, *International Adjudication of Human Rights and the European Court of Human Rights: A Survey of Its Procedural and Some of its Substantive Holdings*, 7 GA. J. INT'L & COMP. L. 315, 377–408 (1977).

> In sum, the Court considers that the intervention of one organ satisfies Article 5(4), but on condition that the procedure followed has a judicial character and gives to the individual concerned guarantees appropriate to the kind of deprivation of liberty in question. . . .
>
> The forms of the procedure required by the Convention need not, however, necessarily be identical in each of the cases where the intervention of a court is required. In order to determine whether a proceeding provides adequate guarantees, regard must be had to the particular nature of the circumstances in which such proceeding takes place. . . .
>
> [In the Vagrancy cases, decisions to detain vagrants were taken by magistrates but were considered under Belgian law to be administrative rather than judicial acts.] The procedure in question is affected by the administrative nature of the decision to be given. It does not ensure guarantees comparable to those which exist as regards detention in criminal cases, notwithstanding the fact that the detention of vagrants is very similar in many respects. It is hard to understand why persons arrested for simple vagrancy have to be content with such a summary procedure. . . . This procedure undoubtedly presents certain judicial features, such as the hearing taking place and the decision being given in public, but they are not sufficient to give the magistrate the character of a "court" within the meaning of Article 5(4) when due account is taken of the seriousness of what is at stake, namely a long deprivation of liberty [in these cases, from 7 to 21 months] attended by various shameful consequences.[203]

Bodies with only advisory powers, such as Mental Health Review Tribunals or parole boards, cannot be considered a "court" for purposes of article 5(4).[204] However, military tribunals, even if composed of military personnel, may be sufficiently independent in their functions to constitute the required "court".[205]

"Article 5(4) has never been interpreted so as to give the same procedural rights or to imply the same requirements as Article 6(1)," which guarantees the right to a fair trial.[206] "All that Article 5(4) requires is that these proceedings [to challenge detention] should be taken before

---

[203] *Id.* at paras. 75–76, 79–80.

[204] *See, e.g.*, X v. U.K., Eur. Court H.R., note 179 *supra*; Weeks v. U.K., note 560 *infra*; *cf.* Schiesser v. Switzerland, *supra* note 133 and accompanying text.

[205] Engel et al. v. Netherlands, *infra* note 490.

[206] Ireland v. U.K., Eur. Comm. H.R., *supra* note 129, at 580.

a court, and that such remedies should be determined speedily."[207] Thus, exclusion of a detainee and his counsel from proceedings in which the legality of detention is determined does not necessarily violate article 5(4),[208] nor does withholding information in the file from a person detained on the grounds of mental illness (at least where the file is made available to the detainee's lawyer).[209] There is no right of direct (as opposed to indirect) access to a court or to appear in person, but the procedure adopted must contain at least a "minimum adversarial element".[210]

While an initial determination by a court that detention is justified will normally be sufficient,[211] the European Court of Human Rights has required further reviews to continue detention on the grounds of mental illness[212] or in order to revoke parole.[213]

In the context of a habeas corpus petition brought to challenge detention while awaiting deportation, however, the European Commission on Human Rights did not require judicial review of the underlying facts on which the detention was based. Review of "the statutory basis for the applicant's detention and whether there were reasonable grounds for the Secretary of State to consider that the applicant was an illegal entrant" was held to be sufficient.[214]

---

[207]X v. Austria, App. No. 8201/78, Eur. Comm. H.R., dec. on admissibility of 17 Mar. 1981, *reprinted in* 1 STRASBOURG DIGEST 589.

[208]X v. Switzerland, App. No. 8485/79, Eur. Comm. H.R., dec. on admissibility of 17 Mar. 1981, 22 Dec. & Rep. 131 (citing the Court's decision in the Neumeister case, *supra* note 153).

[209]X v. Belgium, App. No. 6859/74, Eur. Comm. H.R., dec. on admissibility of 2 Oct. 1975, 3 Dec. & Rep. 139.

[210]Sanchez-Reisse v. Switzerland, App. No. 9862/82, Eur. Court H.R., Judgment of 21 Oct. 1986, Ser. A No. 107. However, a concurring opinion of two judges rejected the majority's suggestion that an exclusively written procedure would be sufficient under art. 5(4):

> [I]t seems to us that this provision is fully satisfied only if the detainee has an opportunity to be heard in person. The Article in question is based on the institution of *habeas corpus*, which is based on the principle that the person concerned appears in flesh and blood before the court.
>
> Such a view is moreover consistent with previous decisions of the Court, which has hitherto tended—as the judgment points out—to recognise the need for a court hearing. Admittedly, the case-law so far concerns only the eventualities contemplated in sub-paragraphs (c) [arrest on suspicion of having committed a crime] and (e) [detention to prevent disease or of the mentally ill, alcoholics, drug addicts, or vagrants] . . . , but we see no reason why it should not also apply [in the circumstances of extradition].

[211]"Article 5(1)(a) is a mere formal requirement which justifies the detention of a person convicted by a competent court. The detention is ordered as a retributive punishment for the immutable fact that the person concerned has been found guilty of an offence. Therefore the grounds on which the decision to convict and sentence were taken are not, unlike the case of a person of unsound mind, subject to change during detention." X v. U.K., App. No. 9089/80, Eur. Comm. H.R., dec. on admissibility of 9 Dec. 1980, 24 Dec. & Rep. 227, 228–29.

[212]*See* discussion *supra* at 38–42.

[213]*See* discussion *infra* at 125–30.

[214]Zamir v. U.K., *supra* note 164. *Compare* Ireland v. U.K., *supra* note 129, in which judicial review of emergency powers of arrest in Northern Ireland was considered *not* to be compatible with article 5(4) if limited to considering bad faith, absence of a genuine suspicion, improper motive, or

A fundamental component of the right to have the legality of detention judged by a court is that such judgment be provided "speedily"[215] or "without delay";[216] indeed, under the European system, the importance of this requirement has been cited as the rationale which permits the proceedings to deviate from normal fair trial standards.

> [Article 5(4)] lays down that such remedies must be determined "speedily". . . . This clearly indicates what the main concern must be in this matter. Full written proceedings or an oral hearing of the parties in the examination of such remedies would be a source of delay which it is important to avoid in this field.[217]

While an early European case held that a hearing within three months of arrest was sufficient to meet the requirements of a speedy determination,[218] it is doubtful that such a long delay would today be considered to be permissible. Subsequent cases involving delays of several months have been found to violate the requirement that determinations be made "speedily,"[219] and the European Commission on Human Rights has stated that, at least in the context of military discipline, a period of even one month for a final determination of the legality of detention exceeds the mandate of article 5(4).[220] Final decisions after 10 and 16 days, in circumstances where the applicant had already been legally detained for many years, have been upheld as consistent with the Convention's requirements.[221]

In the context of persons detained "with a view to deportation or extradition," the European Commission has stated that "only the existence of extradition [or deportation] proceedings justifies deprivation of liberty in such a case. It follows that if, for example, the proceedings are not conducted with the requisite diligence or if the detention results from some misuse of authority, it ceases to be justifiable. . . . "[222]

---

failure to comply with statutory procedures – but excluding consideration of the reasonableness or fairness of the suspicion on which arrest was based or the decision to exercise the powers.

[215]European, art. 5(4).

[216]CivPol, art. 9(4); American, art. 7(6).

[217]*See, e.g.*, Neumeister v. Austria, *supra* note 153, at 43–44.

[218]X v. F.R.G., App. No. 4833/71, Eur. Comm. H.R., dec. on admissibility of 19 July 1971, 38 Coll. Dec. 130.

[219]*See, e.g.*, Sanchez-Reisse v. Switzerland, *supra* note 210 [two separate periods of 31 days and 46 days]; Zamir v. U.K., *supra* note 164 [4½ months]; Luberti v. Italy, *supra* note 175 [18 months' delay]; Van Droogenbroeck v. Belgium, *supra* note 105 [6 months].

[220]Engel et al. v. Netherlands, *infra* note 490.

[221]Christinet v. Switzerland, App. No. 7648/76, Eur. Comm. H.R., Report of 1 Mar. 1979, 17 Dec. & Rep. 35.

[222]Lynas v. Switzerland, App. No. 7317/75, Eur. Comm. H.R., dec. on admissibility of 6 Oct. 1976, 20 Y.B. EUR. CONV. ON HUMAN RIGHTS 412, 442. One of the few violations found in this context was in Sanchez-Reisse v. Switzerland, *supra* note 210.

A somewhat curious corollary of the focus on timeliness is that a person detained for a period which would clearly be permissible under the Convention may have no right to be brought before a court if he or she is released prior to expiration of the shortest time period within which the lawfulness of detention could be examined.[223] Since a person subsequently expelled might be unable to avail himself of the Convention's machinery, it would seem that a wholly illegal and unjustifiable detention and expulsion to a non-Convention country might be beyond the effective reach of article 5's prohibition against arbitrary detention, so long as the expelling state acted with sufficient alacrity.[224]

---

[223]351 X v. Netherlands, Ap. No. 7447/76, Eur. Comm. H.R., dec. on admissibility of 13 Dec. 1976 [2 days in detention prior to expulsion]; X & Y v. Sweden, App. No. 7376/76, Eur. Comm. H.R., dec. on admissibility of 7 Oct. 1976, 7 Dec. & Rep. 123 [2 hours of detention prior to extradition].

[224]Such an "unlawful" detention was found to have occurred when France arrested and expelled a person to Switzerland, whence he was extradited to Italy. The applicant was able to pursue his complaint through the Strasbourg machinery, although the illegality of his arrest and expulsion by French authorities had no impact on his subsequent imprisonment for life in Italy on the basis of an appellate verdict delivered *in absentia*. Bozano v. France, App. No. 9990/82, Eur. Comm. H.R., Report of 7 Dec. 1984. His complaint against Italy was dismissed as beyond the Convention's six-month time limit, Bozano v. Italy, App. No. 9991/82, Eur. Comm. H.R., dec. on admissibility of 12 July 1984, while his complaint against Switzerland, App. No. 9009/80, was withdrawn, following an adverse decision by the European Court of Human Rights on similar facts in Sanchez-Reisse v. Switzerland, *supra* note 210.

EIGHTH AMENDMENT CONCERNS

Cruel and Unusual Punishment

The Eighth Amendment to the U.S. Constitution has an "expansive and vital character" which "is not fastened to the obsolete but may acquire meaning as public opinion becomes enlightened by a humane justice."[225] The international prohibition of "torture" and "cruel, inhuman, or degrading treatment or punishment"[226] is clearly broader than the "cruel and unusual punishment" standard of the Eighth Amendment, at least in its inclusion of "treatment" as well as punishment.[227] The obvious affinity of the international and constitutional standards suggests that the international prohibition might constitute persuasive evidence as to the contemporary meaning of the Eighth Amendment in the United States.

U.S. courts have held that punishment techniques outside the bounds of traditional penalties are "constitutionally suspect"[228] and seem to emphasize the proportionality of the punishment to the crime. For example, the Eighth Amendment is violated by a sentence of fifteen years of

---

[225]Weems v. U.S., 217 U.S. 349 (1910); *cf.*, Trop v. Dulles, 356 U.S. 86, 101 (1958): "The basic concept underlying the Eighth Amendment is nothing less than the dignity of man. . . . The Amendment must draw its meaning from the evolving standards of decency that mark the progress of a maturing society." Similar references to the evolutionary standards of the concept of "degrading punishment" were expressed by the European Court of Human rights in Tyrer v. U.K., App. No. 5856/72, Eur. Court H.R. Judgment of 25 Apr. 1978, Ser. A No. 26, and by the European Commission in the East African Asian Cases, *summarized in* European Commission on Human Rights, *Stock-Taking on the European Convention on Human Rights* 154–56 (1984).

[226]UnivDec, art. 5; CivPol, art. 7; American, art. 5(2); European, art. 3; African, art. 5; Convention against Torture and Other Cruel, Inhuman or Degrading Treatment or Punishment, note 77 *supra*.

[227]"It was generally agreed [during debates in the UN Commission on Human Rights] that the word 'treatment' was broader in scope than the word 'punishment.' " *Annotations of the text on the draft International Covenants on Human Rights, quoted in* M. BOSSUYT, *supra* note 91, at 150. The Eighth Amendment has been held to be applicable only in the criminal justice context. *See, e.g.*, Ingrahm v. Wright, 430 U.S. 651 (1977) (corporal punishment of children in school not included within constitutional protections, although tort remedy may be available). With respect to the right of mental patients to refuse drug treatments, see, *e.g.*, Project Release v. Prevost, 722 F.2d 960 (2d Cir. 1983); Rennie v. Klein, 720 F.2d 266 (3d Cir. 1983).

[228]Trop v. Dulles, *supra* note 225, at 100.

hard labor, while shackled at the ankle and wrist, for falsifying a public document;[229] by denationalization of a soldier absent without leave for one day;[230] by punishing the "disease" of drug addiction;[231] and by imposing the death penalty for rape[232] or, in some circumstances, aiding and abetting a felony.[233] The means used to execute death sentences have thus far survived constitutional challenge.[234] (Other issues of proportionality *re* terms of imprisonment and capital punishment are discussed *infra* at pages 70–71 and 71–77, respectively.)

The international prohibition against torture, at least, now forms part of customary international law which is directly binding upon the United States, as recognized in the oft-cited case of *Filartiga v. Peña-Irala.*[235] In that case, a civil suit brought under the Alien Tort Claims Act[236] for the torture-death of a Paraguayan in Paraguay, the Second Circuit held that the right to be free from torture "has become part of customary law. . . . [and] is now prohibited by the law of nations. The prohibition is clear and unambiguous, and admits of no distinction between treatment of aliens and citizens."[237]

In the case of *Ireland v. U.K.*,[238] in which the Irish government

---

[229]Weems v. U.S., *supra* note 225.

[230]Trop v. Dulles, *supra* note 225.

[231]Robinson v. California, 370 U.S. 660 (1962).

[232]Coker v. Georgia, 433 U.S. 584 (1977).

[233]*Compare* Enmund v. Florida, 458 U.S. 782 (1982) (imposition of capital punishment disproportionate and therefore violative of Eighth Amendment where there is no intent on the part of an aider and abettor that killing take place or lethal force be used) *with* Tison v. Arizona, 107 S. Ct. 1676 (1987) (death penalty permissible in similar felony-murder situation where reckless indifference to life is present, even if defendant did not kill or have any intention to kill).

[234]*See, e.g.*, Glass v. Louisiana, 471 U.S. 1080 (1985) (electrocution); Heckler v. Chaney, 470 U.S. 821 (1985) (Court refused to review Food and Drug Administration decision to refrain from exercising its enforcement power over drugs used in executions by lethal injection); In re Kemmler, 136 U.S. 436 (1890) (electrocution); Wilkerson v. Utah, 99 U.S. 130 (1879) (shooting); Dutton v. State, 123 Md. 373, 91 A. 417 (1914) (hanging).

[235]Note 36 *supra*. While other cases have questioned the availability of the Alien Tort Claims Act as a remedy for violations of international human rights norms, none has questioned the substantive finding of the court in *Filartiga* that torture is prohibited under customary international law. *See, e.g.*, Forti v. Suarez-Mason, 672 F.Supp. 1531 (N.D. Cal. 1987). Among the many articles on this seminal case, see generally Blum & Steinhardt, *Federal Jurisdiction over International Human Rights Claims: The Alien Tort Claims Act after* Filartiga v. Peña-Irala, 22 HARV. INT'L L. J. 53 (1981); Schneebaum, *The Enforceability of Customary Norms of Public International Law*, 8 BROOKLYN J. INT'L L. 289 (1982); discussions in 4 HOUSTON J. INT'L L. (no. 1, 1981). *Cf.* Argentine Republic v. Amerada Hess Shipping Corp., 57 U.S.L.W. 4121 (23 Jan. 1989) (holding that the Foreign Sovereign Immunities Act provides the sole basis for obtaining jurisdiction over a foreign government), *rev'g* 830 F.2d 421 (2d Cir. 1987); Tel-Oren v. Libyan Arab Republic, 726 F.2d 774 (D.C.Cir. 1984), *cert. denied*, 470 U.S. 1003 (1985); Guinto v. Marcos, 654 F.Supp. 276 (S.D.Cal. 1986); Von Dardel v. USSR, 623 F.Supp. 246 (D.D.C. 1985); RESTATEMENT, § 702, especially comment g and Reporters' Note 5.

[236]Note 39 *supra*.

[237]630 F.2d at 883, 884.

[238]Ireland v. U.K., *supra* note 129.

maintained that various practices engaged in by the British in Northern Ireland violated article 3 of the European Convention, the European Court of Human Rights defined torture as "deliberate inhuman treatment causing very serious and cruel suffering."[239] The European Commission of Human Rights had proposed a similar definition in the earlier "Greek Case": torture is "inhuman treatment, which has a purpose, such as the obtaining of information or confessions, or the infliction of punishment, and it is generally an aggravated form of inhuman treatment."[240]

Under the Convention against Torture,

> the term "torture" means any act by which severe pain or suffering, whether physical or mental, is intentionally inflicted on a person for such purposes as obtaining from him or a third person information or a confession, punishing him for an act he or a third person has committed or is suspected of having committed, or intimidating or coercing him or a third person, or for any reason based on discrimination of any kind, when such pain or suffering is inflicted by or at the instigation of or with the consent or acquiescence of a public official or other person acting in an official capacity. It does not include pain or suffering arising only from, inherent in or incidental to lawful sanctions.[241]

The "inhuman" treatment or punishment, of which torture is an aggravated form, has been defined by the European Commission as including "at least such treatment as deliberately causes severe suffering, physical or mental, which in the particular situation is unjustifiable."[242] The

---

[239]Ireland v. U.K., Eur. Court H.R., *supra* note 129, at para. 167.

[240]*Supra* note 161, at para 2.

[241]*Supra* note 77, art. 1. Despite its title, the convention defines only torture and not the other prohibited acts.

A much broader definition may be found in the Inter-American Convention to Prevent and Punish Torture, *adopted* 9 Dec. 1985, O.A.S.T.S. No. 67, O.A.S. Doc. OEA/Ser.P, AG/doc. 2023/85 rev. 1, at 46–54 (1986), 25 INT'L LEGAL MATERIALS 519 (1986):

> [T]orture shall be understood to be any act intentionally performed whereby physical or mental pain or suffering is inflicted on a person for purposes of criminal investigation, as a means of intimidation, as personal punishment, as a preventive measure, as a penalty, or for any other purpose. Torture shall also be understood to be the use of methods upon a person intended to obliterate the personality of the victim or to diminish his physical or mental capacities, even if they do not cause physical pain or mental anguish.
>
> The concept of torture shall not include physical or mental pain or suffering that is inherent in or solely the consequence of lawful measures, provided that they do not include the performance of the acts or use of the methods referred to in this article.

Article 6 of the convention provides that states "shall take effective measures to prevent and punish other cruel, inhuman, or degrading treatment or punishment" but provides no definition of this other prohibited ill-treatment.

[242]Greek Case, *supra* note 161. The Commission subsequently clarified, in Ireland v. U.K., *supra* note 129, at para. 379, that there could never be any justification for the infliction of any treatment contrary to art. 3.

concept of "degrading" treatment or punishment involves the elements of humiliation or debasement; publicity may be a relevant factor, but the Court has made clear that "degrading" treatment within the meaning of the European Convention must be greater than the "usual and perhaps almost inevitable element of humiliation" inherent in any normal judicially prescribed punishment.[243]

The Human Rights Committee adopted a "general comment" on article 7 of the Covenant on Civil and Political Rights, in which it noted:

> It may not be necessary to draw sharp distinctions between the various prohibited forms of treatment or punishment. These distinctions depend on the kind, purpose and severity of the particular treatment. In the view of the Committee the prohibition must extend to corporal punishment, including excessive chastisement as an educational or disciplinary measure. Even such a measure as solitary confinement may, according to the circumstances, and especially when the person is kept incommunicado, be contrary to this article.[244]

All of these concepts are relative, and it is primarily within the European system that attempts have been made to distinguish among the various forms of prohibited ill-treatment. For example, the European Commission held unanimously that the British practice of "interrogation in depth" utilized for a time in Northern Ireland (which included hooding; prolonged wall-standing; constant background noise and light; and deprivation of food, water, and sleep) constituted "torture," while the European Court subsequently downgraded that designation, by a large majority, to "inhuman treatment" in violation of the Convention.[245] Punishment by birching in the Isle of Man was found by the Commission and Court to violate the European Convention's prohibition of "degrading . . . punishment."[246] While the Commission and Court rejected complaints that corporal punishment in English public schools violated article 3 of the Convention, it upheld parental rights to forbid such punishment of their child as a matter of conscience under article 2 of Protocol No. 1 to the Convention.[247]

The Human Rights Committee seems to have reserved findings of a

---

[243]*See* Tyrer v. U.K., *supra* note 225; Campbell & Cosans v. U.K., Eur. Court H.R., Judgment of 25 Feb. 1982, Ser. A No. 48.

[244]Human Rights Committee, General Comment 7 (16) (article 7), *Report of the Human Rights Committee*, *supra* note 138, at 94–95. *See generally* N. RODLEY, THE TREATMENT OF PRISONERS UNDER INTERNATIONAL LAW 71–95 (1987), for a discussion of attempts to define torture and other ill-treatment prohibited under international law; P. SIEGHART, *supra* note 161, at 162–72.

[245]Ireland v. U.K., Eur. Court H.R., *supra* note 129.

[246]Tyrer v. U.K., *supra* note 225.

[247]Campbell & Cosans v. U.K., *supra* note 243.

violation of article 7 for "traditional" physical torture, without distinguishing among the different degrees of ill-treatment.[248] Instances of solitary confinement and incommunicado detention have most often been found to violate article 10's requirement that all detainees be treated "with respect for the inherent dignity of the human person."[249]

Prison Conditions

One of the most effective uses of the Eighth Amendment by U.S. lawyers complaining about abuses in the criminal justice system has been in the area of prison conditions. Scores of state and federal prisons systems have been under court order in recent years to eliminate overcrowding and otherwise improve the conditions in which inmates must live; as of October 1987, 45 states plus the District of Columbia, Puerto Rico, and the U.S. Virgin Islands, were under court order or bound by consent decrees concerning prison conditions.[250]

The U.S. Supreme Court has held that prison conditions, "alone or in combination, may deprive inmates of the minimal civilized measure of life's necessities."[251] Among the conditions which U.S. courts have found could violate the Eighth Amendment are using mattresses on the floor for sleeping,[252] inadequate ventilation,[253] inadequate heating,[254] inadequate lighting,[255] excessive noise,[256] physical deterioration of the prison,[257] inadequate fire protection,[258] and inadequate sanitation.[259]

However, the Court also has stated that specific conditions must inflict "unnecessary or wanton pain" or be "grossly disproportionate to the severity of crimes warranting imprisonment" in order to violate the

---

[248]*See, e.g.*, Angel Estrella v. Uruguay, Comm. No. 74/1980, ***Report of the Human Rights Committee***, 38 UN GAOR, Supp. (No. 40) at 150 (1983); Larrosa v. Uruguay, Comm. No. 88/1981, *id.* at 180; Campora v. Uruguay, Comm. No. 66/1980, *id.* at 117; Vasilskis v. Uruguay, Comm. No. 80/1980, *id.* at 173. One authority has termed the Committee's language in deciding such cases as "especially inconsistent". N. RODLEY, *supra* note 244, at 87.

[249]*See* discussion *infra* at 63–70.

[250]"Status Report: State Prisons and The Courts," J. Nat'l Prison Project (No. 13, Fall 1987) at 24. This list includes the entire prison or jail systems of Alabama, Alaska, Arkansas, Florida, Mississippi, Oklahoma, Rhode Island, South Carolina, Tennessee, Texas, the District of Columbia, and Puerto Rico.

[251]Rhodes v. Chapman, 452 U.S. 337, 347 (1981).

[252]*See, e.g.*, Lareau v. Manson, *supra* note 56.

[253]*See, e.g.*, Blake v. Hall, 668 F.2d 52 (1st Cir. 1981).

[254]Smith v. Sullivan, 553 F.2d 373 (5th Cir. 1977).

[255]*See, e.g.*, Ramos v. Lamm, 639 F.2d 559 (10th Cir. 1980).

[256]*See, e.g.*, Palmigiano v. Garrahy, 442 F. Supp. 956 (D.R.I. 1977).

[257]*See, e.g.*, Grubbs v. Bradley, 552 F. Supp. 1052 (M.D.Tenn. 1982).

[258]*See, e.g.*, French v. Owens, 538 F. Supp. 910 (S.D. Ind. 1982).

[259]*See, e.g.*, Blake v. Hall, *supra* note 253.

Eighth Amendment.[260] For example, the double celling at issue in *Rhodes v. Chapman* was found not to be unconstitutional, as the prison facilities were in good condition and the prisoners adequately protected and treated.

Although they are not legally binding, the most important international norms in this area are the UN Standard Minimum Rules for the Treatment of Prisoners, which were adopted by the Economic and Social Council in 1957.[261] Adopted as guidelines in several U.S. jurisdictions, the Rules set out in detail the minimum rights and facilities which should be made available to prisoners, and they have been cited as evidence of contemporary standards relevant to the scope of the Eighth Amendment's embodiment of "broad and idealistic standards of decency that mark the progress of a maturing society."[262]

Other relevant international standards include the Code of Conduct for Law Enforcement Officials, adopted by the UN General Assembly in 1979,[263] and the Standard Minimum Rules for the Administration of Juvenile Justice ("Beijing Rules"), adopted in 1985.[264] The former reflects many of the concerns addressed in local U.S. police rules and procedures, including requirements for public monitoring of the law enforcement system and the principle of proportionate use of force. The latter is a fairly extensive set of 30 rules, with commentary, which includes both procedural protections and more general principles concerning arrest, investigation, adjudication, and disposition of cases involving juveniles, "intended to be attainable as a policy minimum" in all countries. The UN General Assembly also has adopted a Declaration of Basic Principles of Justice for Victims of Crime and Abuse of Power, which includes recom-

---

[260]Rhodes v. Chapman, *supra* note 251, at 348.

[261]E.S.C. Res. 663C, 24 UN ESCOR, Supp. (No. 1) at 11, UN Doc. E/3048 (1957), *extended,* E.S.C. Res. 2976(LXII), 62 UN ESCOR, Supp. (No. 1) at 35 (1977), *reprinted in* R. LILLICH, *supra* note 16, at 450.1. *See generally, e.g.*, Toman, *Quasi-Legal Standards and Guidelines for Protecting Human Rights of Detained Persons*, in GUIDE TO INTERNATIONAL HUMAN RIGHTS PRACTICE 201–09 (H. Hannum ed. 1984); Skoler, *World Implementation of the United Nations Standard Minimum Rules for Treatment of Prisoners*, 10 J. INT'L L. & ECON. 453 (1975).

[262]Estelle v. Gamble, 429 U.S. 97, 102–03 (1976); see also Hutto v. Finney, 434 U.S. 689 (1978); Weems v. U.S., *supra* note 225; Sostre v. McGinnins, 442 F.2d 178 (2d Cir. 1971); Holt v. Sarver, 442 F.2d 304 (8th Cir. 1968); Jackson v. Bishop, 404 F.2d 571 (8th Cir. 1968). Among cases specifically citing the Rules, see, *e.g.*, Lareau v. Manson, note 56 *supra*, at 106 n.6, *aff'g* 507 F.Supp. 1177 (D.Conn. 1980); Morgan v. La Vallee, 526 F.2d 221, 226 n.8 (2d Cir. 1975); Detainees of Brooklyn House of Detention for Men v. Malcom, 520 F.2d 392 (2d Cir. 1975); Sterling v. Cupp, 290 Or. 611, 622 n.21, 625 P.2d 123, 131 n.21 (1981); and cases cited in R. LILLICH, *supra* note 16, at 450.14.

[263]G.A. Res. 34/169, 34 UN GAOR, Supp. (No. 46) at 185, Annex (1979), *reprinted in* UNITED NATIONS, A COMPILATION OF INTERNATIONAL INSTRUMENTS 226–32 (1988).

[264]G.A. RES. 40/33, 40 UN GAOR, Supp. (No. 53) at 206, Annex (1985), *reprinted in* UN COMPILATION, *supra* note 263, at 237–61.

mendations regarding access to justice, restitution, compensation, and assistance to victims.[265]

The issue of prison conditions has been raised in several applications before the European Commission of Human Rights, notably in the Greek Case[266] and several applications concerning members of the Baader-Meinhof terrorist group in Germany.[267]

> [I]n assessing whether such a measure may fall within the ambit of Article 3 . . . , regard must be had to the particular conditions, the stringency of the measure, its duration, the objective pursued and its effects on the person concerned. Complete sensory isolation coupled with complete social isolation can no doubt ultimately destroy the personality; thus it constitutes a form of inhuman treatment which cannot be justified by the requirements of security. . . .[268]

In the Baader-Meinhof cases, however, the Commission found no evidence that the applicants were "deliberately subjected to a range of physical or mental suffering designed to punish them, to destroy their personality or to break down their resistance," and thus no violation of article 3.[269]

Several other applications have challenged restrictions on a prisoner's normal contacts with other prisoners and the outside world, but no violation of the Convention has been found on the facts of the particular cases (most of which provided for partial isolation of the prisoner but permitted limited visits from relatives and lawyers).[270] Even where the Commission criticized disciplinary punishments which included, *inter alia*, seven days of "sleeping hard" and a diet consisting only of bread and "the usual beverage," as "no longer corresponding to modern standards,"

---

[265]G.A. Res. 40/34, 40 UN GAOR, Supp. (No. 53) at 213, Annex, *reprinted in* UN COMPILATION, *supra* note 263, at 262–65.

[266]Note 161 *supra*; a good summary of the issues related to conditions of detention may be found in N. RODLEY, *supra* note 244, at 223–26.

[267]Apps. Nos. 5874/72, 6038/73, 6166/73, 7572/76, 7586/76 & 7587/76, summarized in *Stock-Taking, supra* note 225, at 58–60. Also see McFeeley v. U.K., note 275 *infra* ("H block" prisoners in Northern Ireland); Kirkwood v. U.K., discussed *infra* note 300 and accompanying text.

[268]Ensslin, Baader & Raspe v. F.R.G., Apps. Nos 7572/76, 7586/76 & 7587/76, Eur. Comm. H.R., dec. on admissibility of 8 July 1978, 14 Dec. & Rep. 64, 109.

[269]*Id.* at 111.

[270]*See, e.g.*, Krocher & Moller v. Switzerland, *infra* note 272 (decreasing stages of isolation and surveillance over 10 ½ months); Reed v. U.K., App. No. 7630/76, Eur. Comm. H.R., Report of 17 Dec. 1981, 19 Dec. & Rep. 113 (12 weeks solitary confinement); X v. Denmark, App. No. 8395/78, Eur. Comm. H.R., dec. on admissibility of 16 Dec. 1981, 27 Dec. & Rep. 50 (15 months isolation during detention on remand); De Courcy v. U.K., App. 2749/66, Eur. Comm. H.R., partial dec. on admissibility of 16 Dec. 1966, 10 Y.B. EUR. CONV. ON HUMAN RIGHTS 382 (10 months solitary confinement). For a highly critical view of the use of "dissociation" and "administrative segregation" in Canada, see M. JACKSON, PRISONERS OF ISOLATION: SOLITARY CONFINEMENT IN CANADA (1983).

it declined to find that the treatment was "inhuman or degrading" within the prohibition of the European Convention.[271]

An application decided by the Commission in 1982 is illustrative of the Commission's approach in such cases.[272] The applicants were suspected (and subsequently convicted) terrorists, and their complaints concerned the period of ten and one-half months prior to trial when they were held in varying degrees of isolation.

> Having regard, firstly, to the circumstances in which the applicants were arrested . . . and, secondly, to the life history of the two applicants, . . . there were undoubtedly compelling reasons in this case for holding both applicants in conditions more especially geared to security considerations.
>
> As it is clear from the establishment of the facts, the applicants' isolation—in particular their accommodation in non-adjacent cells on a floor not occupied by other prisoners and with no opening on to the outside world—the constant artificial lighting, permanent surveillance by closed-circuit television, the denial of access to newspapers and radio and the lack of physical exercise, were the most striking characteristics of the prison conditions imposed upon them.
>
> It is true that these general conditions were subsequently altered as a result of various appeals and suits by the applicants or interventions by doctors. . . .
>
> The respondent Government has repeatedly stated that the sole purpose of the special conditions of detention to which the applicants were subjected was to ensure security inside and outside the prison. The applicants were dangerous people and it was accepted from the start that there was a risk of escape and collusion. These specific measures were not therefore taken with punitive intent, nor were they intended, as the applicants maintain, "to enable their personalities and behaviour to be constantly supervised and their integrity and identities to be destroyed". . .
>
> The question that arises is whether the balance between the requirements of security and basic individual rights was not disrupted to the detriment of the latter. The Commission is therefore required to examine the security measures one by one and the effect produced or likely to be produced by their temporary or long-term combination, so that it can judge whether these measures, which the Swiss authorities gradually altered,

[271]*See* X v. F.R.G., App. No. 7408/76, Eur. Comm. H.R., dec. on admissibility of 11 July 1977, 10 Dec. & Rep. 221.

[272]Krocher & Moller v. Switzerland, App. No. 8463/78, Eur. Comm. H.R., Report of 16 Dec. 1982.

were likely to create conditions of detention attaining a level of severity that could constitute a violation of Article 3 of the Convention.

In other words the Commission must decide whether the prison conditions imposed on the applicants, in which they were undeniably held in almost total isolation, constituted treatment that could be described as inhuman or degrading. . . .

In this respect the Commission has already had occasion to recall that the segregation of a prisoner from the prison community does not in itself constitute a form of inhuman treatment. . . .

It has on other occasions stated that complete sensory isolation coupled with total social isolation, can destroy the personality and constitutes a form of treatment which cannot be justified by the requirements of security or any other reason. . . .

In making an assessment in a given case, regard must be had to the surrounding circumstances including the particular conditions, the stringency of the measure, its duration, the objective pursued and its effects on the person concerned. . . .

The general situation that the climate of terrorism had reached in the autumn of 1977 also needs to be emphasised. The facts relating to the present application were preceded by dramatic events [including a political kidnapping, the hijacking of an aircraft, and the deaths in prison of three members of the Baader-Meinhof group in the Federal Republic of Germany]. . . . It follows that the attitude of the Swiss authorities, in particular their concern to keep the applicants under extremely close supervision, has also to be seen in this respect as a measure to protect their lives and physical integrity. . . .

[T]he Commission cannot conclude that the prison, the part of the building in which the applicants were held or their individual cells could have given rise to sensory isolation amounting to a form of treatment which could not be justified by the security requirements. . . . [The Commission also rejected allegations that the social isolation to which the prisoners were subjected was impermissible, noting the regular medical examinations, permission for the prisoners to receive regular visits from lawyers and close relatives, correspondence, and ability to read books during detention.]

As regards the *severity* of the measures ordered, the Commission would point out that the applicants were placed in isolation only for the first month of their detention. From the end of January onwards they were able to confer with their lawyers and see their families.

> A further fact to emphasise is that the Swiss authorities gradually relaxed the conditions in which the applicants were detained. In particular, the measure relating to continuous artificial lighting was very quickly revoked [after two months], and the ban on newspapers and radio was lifted after the Federal Court . . . had declared this measure illegal [after nearly six months]. . . .
>
> On the *effects* of the conditions of detention, the Commission cannot, in the light of the information available to it and in particular the medical reports, conclude that those conditions could, according to the Commission's agreed criteria, "destroy the personality and cause severe mental and physical suffering" to the applicants. . . .
>
> The Commission therefore considers that the special conditions imposed on the applicants could not be construed as inhuman or degrading treatment within the meaning of Article 3 of the Convention.[273]

The majority view was adopted by a vote of only eight to five, and four of the dissenters wrote a minority opinion:

> Our position is that closer attention should have been paid to the situation imposed on the applicants during the first month of their detention and to consider this in the light of Article 3. From this standpoint we consider that if the criteria that emerge from the case-law of the Commission and the Court are applied to this period alone, then the situation in question must be regarded as contrary to Article 3. We do not think that conditions of detention of such severity have ever been brought to the Commission's notice in the past. The fact that a situation prohibited by Article 3 was gradually relaxed does not mean that that situation can be justified retroactively in regard to that provision.
>
> It is clear that new threats to public order, the State and even individuals have arisen in our communities in modern times, and that these threats are unacceptable in a democratic framework. Consequently, it is vital that new measures be taken to defend the State, the individual and, more generally, the very essence of a democratic state.
>
> These requirements demand a new approach: the State and the authorities must cope with . . . such problems, but we consider that the manner in which this is done must be *compatible* with the legitimate object of these measures (or this ap-

---

[273]*Id.* at 15–22; references omitted; emphasis in original.

> proach), in the light of the Convention and the fundamental principles of our democracies; the purpose of taking these measures . . . is to defend a democratic state and the rights of other individuals, but they may not be ordered or implemented in such a way that the *rights of offenders, as set out in the Convention, are not or cannot be respected.*
>
> It is clear that the applicants were particularly dangerous people and that particularly rigorous arrangements had to be made for their detention in order to ensure the security of the prison authorities and the physical integrity of the applicants, to eliminate any risk of escape and guarantee their appearance before the investigating and prosecuting authorities.
>
> The security measures adopted in regard to them no doubt comply with these objectives which are in themselves legitimate. However we consider that there has to be proportionality between the satisfaction of these demands and the respect due to every human being, however dangerous.
>
> In our opinion, this balance was not achieved in the circumstances of the present case. The measures initially adopted and the arrangements subsequently made, although having the effect of relaxing the initial conditions of detention, cannot be justified under the Convention. Neither the fact that, in the case of the applicants, Switzerland was confronted with terrorists for the first time, nor the publicity surrounding the deaths of [members of the Baader-Meinhof group] . . . can justify these measures even though they help to explain the reaction of the Swiss authorities.[274]

The issue of prison conditions, as opposed to isolation, was addressed in a case involving the so-called "dirty protest" by I.R.A. members imprisoned in Northern Ireland.[275] While highly critical of the British Government's handling of the protest, the European Commission of Human Rights found that the prisoners had themselves contributed to the deterioration of the conditions—confinement to cells, since the prisoners refused to wear prison clothing; smearing of excrement on cell walls; and removal of mattresses and bedding from the cells during the daytime—and that there was consequently no violation of the Convention's norms.

Article 10 of the Covenant on Civil and Political Rights requires more specifically that "all persons deprived of their liberty shall be treated with

---

[274]*Id.* at 23–24 (dissenting op. of MM. Tenekides, Melchior, Sampaio, and Weitzel); emphasis in original.

[275]McFeeley and others v. U.K., App. No. 8317/78, Eur. Comm. H.R., dec. on admissibility of 15 May 1980, 20 Dec. & Rep. 44.

humanity and with respect for the inherent dignity of the human person." The Human Rights Committee's "general comment" on this article underscores its importance and its application to all situations in which individuals are confined against their will (*e.g.*, hospitals, detention camps, or correctional institutions).[276] It has found that this article is violated by keeping prisoners in small, rudimentary cells with constant electric light;[277] by generally inadequate prison conditions;[278] and by the mere fact of incommunicado or solitary confinement for extended periods of time.[279]

The Covenant on Civil and Political Rights and American Convention on Human Rights specifically require that accused persons be separated from convicted prisoners (except in exceptional circumstances) and that juveniles be segregated from adults.[280] Upon his submission of these two treaties to the Senate for its advice and consent, President Carter indicated that the U.S. considered these provisions "as goals to be achieved progressively rather than through immediate implementation."[281]

Sentencing

Early in its jurisprudence, the European Commission stated that "the [European] Convention does not provide as such any general right to call into question the length of a sentence imposed by a competent court."[282] Subsequent cases do not seem to be quite so categorical,[283] and the Commission has noted that "issues may arise under Article 3 in relation to

---

[276]Human Rights Committee, General Comment 9 (16) (article 10), *Report of the Human Rights Committee*, *supra* note 138, at 96–97.

[277]*See, e.g.*, Larrosa v. Uruguay, *supra* note 138; Manera v. Uruguay, Comm. No. 123/1982, *Report of the Human Rights Committee*, 39 UN GAOR, Supp. (No. 40) at 175 (1984).

[278]*See, e.g.*, Wight v. Madagascar, Comm. No. 115/1982, *Report of the Human Rights Committee*, 40 UN GAOR, Supp. (No. 40) at 171 (1985); Arzuaga v. Uruguay, Comm. No. 147/1983, *Report of the Human Rights Committee*, 41 UN GAOR, Supp. (No. 40) at 128 (1986).

[279]*See, e.g.*, Drescher v. Uruguay, Comm. No. 43/1979, *Report of the Human Rights Committee* (1983), *supra* note 248, at 192 [6 weeks incommunicado detention]; Magana ex-Philibert v. Zaire, Comm. No. 90/1981, *id.* at 197 [9 months]; Martinez v. Uruguay, Comm. No. 83/1981, *Report of the Human Rights Committee* (1984), *supra* note 277, at 148 [over 5 months]; Conteris v. Uruguay, Comm. No. 139/1983, *Report of the Human Rights Committee* (1985), *supra* note 278, at 196 [over three months]; Arzuaga v. Uruguay, *supra* note 278 [15 days].

[280]CivPol, art. 19(2); American, art. 5(4) & (5).

[281]Message of the President Transmitting Four Treaties Pertaining to Human Rights, *supra* note 20, at xii, xviii. The President's Message specifically recognizes that the American Convention and Covenant on Civil and Political Rights set forth standards of treatment which U.S. practice does not yet meet. *Id.*

[282]X v. U.K., App. No. 5871/72, Eur. Comm. H.R., dec. on admissibility of 30 Sept. 1974, 1 Dec. & Rep. 54, 55; also see X v. F.R.G., App. No. 1650/62, Eur. Comm. H.R., dec. on admissibility of 7 Mar. 1964 (unpublished).

[283]*See, e.g.*, X v. U.K., App. No. 8081/77, Eur. Comm. H.R., dec. on admissibility of 12 Dec. 1977, 12 Dec. & Rep. 207; X v. U.K., App. No. 7706/67, Eur. Comm. H.R., dec. on admissibility of 5 Oct. 1977 (unpublished); X v. F.R.G., Eur. Comm. H.R., dec. on admissibility of 13 May 1976, 6 Dec. & Rep. 127.

any lawful sentence of imprisonment as regards the manner of its execution and its length,"[284] as when "an exceptionally harsh punishment for a trivial offence" is imposed.[285]

No sentence of itself has yet been found to violate article 3 of the Convention, but the Commission has suggested that sentences of life imprisonment should be subject to review by the appropriate national authorities (although no such review is mandated by the European Convention).[286] The most direct reference to excessive punishment is found in *Weeks v. U.K.*, in which the European Court of Human Rights suggested that a sentence of life imprisonment for a minor robbery would raise "serious doubts" as to its compatibility with article 3's prohibition against inhuman punishment.[287]

The U.S. Supreme Court has been similarly reluctant to inquire into the proportionality of punishment, except with respect to imposition of life sentences without possibility of parole and the death penalty.[288] In *Solem v. Helm*,[289] the Court held that a life sentence without possibility of parole for a defendant convicted of his seventh nonviolent felony was unconstitutional. A five-justice majority identified the following criteria to guide the court's proportionality analysis under the Eighth Amendment: balancing the gravity of the offense and the harshness of the penalty; comparing the challenged sentence with sentences imposed on other criminals in the same jurisdiction; and comparing the sentence imposed with sentences for commission of the same crime in other jurisdictions.[290]

Capital Punishment

The convoluted history of the Supreme Court, the death penalty, due

---

[284]Kotalla v. Netherlands, App. No. 6994/77, Eur. Comm. H.R., dec. on admissibility of 6 May 1978, 14 Dec. & Rep. 238, 240.

[285]X v. U.K., App. No. 5471/72, Eur. Comm. H.R., dec. on admissibility of 9 Feb. 1973, 43 Coll. Dec. 160.

[286]Kotalla v. Netherlands, *supra* note 284, at 240–41.

[287]*Infra* note 560, at para. 47. The partly dissenting opinion of Judge de Meyer stated that a life sentence in such circumstances "would have exceeded any reasonable relationship of proportionality with what actually happened. It would have been what the Eighth Amendment to the Constitution of the United States of America calls 'cruel and unusual punishment,' and what Article 3 of the European Convention on Human Rights terms 'inhuman punishment.' "

[288]However, see Weems v. U.S., *supra* note 225, in which the court condemned the punishment as excessive in comparison to the crime committed, as well as inherently cruel; W. LAFAVE & J. SCOTT, *supra* note 93, at 179, 181–82.

[289]463 U.S. 277 (1983).

[290]*Id.* at 292. *Compare* Hutto v. Davis, 454 U.S. 370 (1982) (upholding 40-year sentence for possession of nine ounces of marijuana with intent to distribute) and Rummel v. Estelle, 445 U.S. 263 (1980) (upholding life imprisonment *with* possibility of parole for recidivist after conviction for third minor felony).

process, and the Eighth Amendment need not be repeated here.[291] While the major international human rights conventions do permit imposition of the death penalty, most impose stringent limitations on its use and specifically provide that it may not be reintroduced in a country which has abolished it. Among the various limitations are that the death penalty may not be imposed on persons who were under 18 or over 70 at the time they committed a crime, or on pregnant women; that a condemned person has the right to seek pardon or commutation; and that the death penalty may be imposed "only for the most serious crimes" and "pursuant to a final judgment rendered by a competent court."[292] In 1984, the UN Economic and Social Council adopted a set of "safeguards guaranteeing protection of the rights of those facing the death penalty," which was subsequently endorsed by the Seventh UN Congress on the Prevention of Crime and the Treatment of Offenders.[293]

While most countries currently do impose capital punishment, there seems to be a growing international trend towards abolition.[294] Protocol No. 6 to the European Convention on Human Rights, which entered into force in 1985, abolishes the death penalty in peacetime,[295] and a second Optional Protocol to the Covenant on Civil and Political Rights, which also would abolish the death penalty, is currently being considered.[296] Among countries for which information is available, 41 have legally abolished the death penalty;[297] two are abolitionist in practice; nine have had no executions for the past ten years; and 115 retain the death penalty.[298] Among

---

[291]Among recent Supreme Court cases dealing with the death penalty, see, *e.g.*, Thompson v. Oklahoma, *infra* note 307; Tison v. Arizona, *supra* note 233; Spaziano v. Florida, 468 U.S. 447 (1984); Enmund v. Florida, *supra* note 233; Eddings v. Oklahoma, 455 U.S. 104 (1982); Coker v. Georgia, *supra* note 232; Gregg v. Georgia, 428 U.S. 153 (1976); Furman v. Georgia, 408 U.S. 238 (1972).

[292]CivPol, art. 6; American, art. 4; European, art. 2. The U.S. proposed reservations to these provisions in the Civil and Political Covenant and American Convention, Message of the President, *supra* note 20, at xii, xviii.

[293]ESC Res. 1984/50 of 24 May 1984, *reprinted in* UN COMPILATION, note 263 *supra*, at 236–37; *cf.* Committee on Crime Prevention and Control, *Implementation of the United Nations safeguards guaranteeing protection of the rights of those facing the death penalty*, UN Doc. E/AC.57/1988/9 (1988).

[294]*See generally* F. ZIMRING AND G. HAWKINS, CAPITAL PUNISHMENT AND THE AMERICAN AGENDA 3–25 (1986); *Analysis Concerning the Proposition to Elaborate a Second Optional Protocol to the International Covenant on Civil and Political Rights, aiming at the Abolition of the Death Penalty* (M. Bossuyt, Special Rapporteur), UN Doc. E/CN,.4/Sub.2/1987/20 (1987).

[295]Of the 21 members of the Council of Europe, only Cyprus, Greece, Ireland, and Turkey imposed the death penalty for non-military offenses at the time the Protocol was signed in 1983. *See* Council of Europe, Press Release I(83)29, 28 Apr. 1983.

[296]*Cf.* Bossuyt, *supra* note 294.

[297]Of these, 12 retain the possibility of capital punishment in wartime or under other exceptional circumstances.

[298]Bossuyt, *supra* note 294, at 19–20. As of 1 Dec. 1987, a record 1,984 prisoners were on death row in 34 states, according to the Bureau of Justice Statistics. "25 Prisoners Were Executed Last Year, Justice Dept. Says," Wash. Post, 1 Aug. 1988, at A4, col. 1.

Western countries, only the United States retains capital punishment in peacetime.[299]

The death penalty as applied in the United States has been considered by two regional human rights bodies, in connection with conditions on "death row" and the execution of juvenile offenders.

A U.S. citizen arrested in the United Kingdom challenged his extradition to California on the grounds, *inter alia*, that he would be subject to the death penalty if convicted, despite an assurance from California that the British government's opposition to imposition of the death penalty would be brought to the attention of the appropriate authorities.[300] The applicant did not challenge the death penalty *per se*, which is permitted under article 2 of the European Convention, but rather asserted that conditions on death row amounted to inhuman and degrading treatment contrary to article 3 of the Convention.

> The applicant complains . . . that the 'assurance', that the United Kingdom's wish that he should not be executed will be brought to the Governor's attention, will only operate after he has completed all possible appeals and that in the interval he will be exposed to the rigours of the death row phenomenon. . . .
>
> The applicant does not contend that the death penalty as such would constitute inhuman and degrading treatment contrary to Article 3; he argues however that the circumstances surrounding the implementation of such a death penalty, and in particular the "death row" phenomenon, of excessive delay during a prolonged appeal procedure lasting several years, during which he would be gripped with uncertainty as to the outcome of his appeal and therefore his fate, would constitute inhuman and degrading treatment. . . .
>
> In these circumstances, faced with an imminent act of the [British] executive the consequences of which for the applicant will allegedly expose him to Article 3 treatment, the Commission finds that the applicant is able to claim to be a victim of an alleged violation of Article 3. It remains for the Commission to consider whether or not the matters alleged by the applicant to constitute treatment contrary to Article 3 are of such seriousness as to fall within the ambit of that provision.
>
> The Commission has recognised in its previous case law that a person's extradition may, exceptionally, give rise to issues under Article 3 of the Convention where extradition is contem-

---

[299]Liechtenstein also formally provides for capital punishment, but no one has been executed since 1785. Bossuyt, *supra* note 294, at 20.

[300]Kirkwood v. U.K., App. No. 10479/83, Eur. Comm. H.R., dec. on admissibility of 12 Mar. 1984.

plated to a country in which "due to the very nature of the regime of that country or to a particular situation in the country, basic human rights, such as are guaranteed by the Convention, might be either grossly violated or entirely suppressed". . . .

The respondent Government contend that . . . any delay arising as a result of the opportunities for appeal and legal control of the imposition of a death penalty as a result of a conviction is implicitly foreseen by Article 2(1) of the Convention, and thus cannot constitute inhuman and degrading treatment contrary to Article 3.

The Commission cannot accept this contention. . . . [T]he Convention organs must be reluctant to draw inferences from one text which would restrict the express terms of another.

As both the Court and the Commission have recognised, Article 3 is not subject to any qualification. Its terms are bald and absolute. . . .

The Commission must therefore consider the nature of the treatment which the applicant complains he would be subjected to in the event of his extradition, and the severity of the risk thereby arising, in order to assess whether or not it attains a sufficient degree of seriousness to raise an issue under Article 3 of the Convention. . . .

On the basis of the information before it, the Commission considers the probability that the applicant, if convicted, will be sentenced to death is high, although it cannot prejudge this issue which will depend upon the outcome of the proceedings. In any case, the Commission finds that the risk is sufficiently real and immediate to justify its examination of other aspects of the seriousness of the treatment to which the applicant contends that he will be subjected. . . .

The overall delays [in the appeal system] are severe. From figures submitted by the applicant, as of March 1983, 115 persons are awaiting execution in California, and 1147 in the United States as a whole. . . . [T]he average amount of time between the entry of a death judgment and its reversal, vacation or affirmation by the Supreme Court of California has up to now been two years, although several cases required four years for their resolution. However in the applicant's contention this period is lengthening, because there is a growing backlog of accumulated cases awaiting judgment from the Supreme Court of California. . . . [[301]]

[301]In the four states with the highest number of executions in the post-*Furman* period (Texas, Florida, Louisiana, and Georgia), the average time between the date of crime and execution ranged from 5 years, 9 months, in Louisiana to 9 years and 11 months in Georgia. Information supplied by the Circuit Executive for the Eleventh Circuit Court of Appeals (as of March 1988); on file with author.

[The Commission then found that the assurances given to Kirkwood did not amount to a legal guarantee that any death sentence would be commuted and that, in any event, such an assurance is not expressly or implicitly required by article 3.]

For the following reasons the Commission considers that, grave though the risk and the treatment which the applicant is likely to endure are, they do not attain the degree of seriousness envisaged by Article 3 of the Convention.

First the Commission notes the existence of complex and detailed measures to accelerate the appeal system in capital cases in California. . . . It is true that delays subsist in dealing with appeals under the automatic appeal procedure in California, but the Commission cannot lose sight of the momentous significance of these appeals for the particular appellant in each case, whose life depends upon the outcome. . . .

[I]t is established that the death row phenomenon is now an arguable basis for alleging cruel or unusual punishment in the United States, and [the Commission] cannot ignore the similarity between this concept and that of inhuman and degrading treatment under Article 3 of the Convention. . . . [I]t must be regarded as likely, if convicted, that the applicant will be exposed to the death row phenomenon. However this cannot be presupposed as a fact, and it is significant that the applicant will have a fair trial conforming with guarantees equivalent to those contained in the Convention before any decision is reached which would result in his being on death row.

It is not the Commission's task . . . to assess as a mathematical probability the likelihood of the applicant being exposed to the treatment about which he complains, but to examine the machinery of justice to which he will be subjected and to establish whether there are any aggravating factors which might indicate arbitrariness or unreasonableness in its operation. . . . [Finding no such factors,] the Commission does not find that the delays in the operation of the death penalty in California as they may apply to the applicant constitute a "particular situation" of the kind envisaged in [earlier cases]. . . . [There also is nothing to show] that the conditions of detention of death row prisoners are so severe as to constitute a gravely aggravating aspect in assessing the seriousness of the applicant's complaints. . . .

It follows that this aspect of the application is manifestly ill-founded. . . . [302]

---

[302] *Id.* at 3, 26–37. Kirkwood subsequently pled guilty in California to second degree murder and received a sentence of 15 years to life, with the possibility of parole after 7½ years.

The Inter-American Commission considered a case against the United States which challenged the execution of juvenile offenders.[303] In essence, the petitioners argued that the Commission should interpret the American Declaration of the Rights and Duties of Man in a manner consistent with contemporary customary international law which, petitioners submitted, prohibited the execution of minors.[304] The United States noted, *inter alia*, that the American Declaration did not directly address the issue of capital punishment and denied, in any event, that customary international law prohibited juvenile executions generally or recognition of eighteen as the age of majority.

The Commission decided the case on its merits, even though the two petitioners—James Terry Roach and Jay Pinkerton—were executed during the course of the proceedings, after having exhausted their domestic appeals. The Commission agreed that, even if there were a customary international law norm against the execution of juvenile offenders, the United States would not be legally bound by such a norm in light of its persistent objections. In addition, it was "convinced by the U.S. Government's argument that there does not now exist a norm of customary international law establishing 18 to be the minimum age for imposition of the death penalty."[305] However, the Commission went on to hold that there does exist a peremptory norm of international law, or *jus cogens*, to which no objection is possible, against the execution of juvenile offenders. Even if the precise age limit was unclear, the failure of the U.S. to protect against such executions violated U.S. obligations under the American Declaration.

> The Commission finds that the diversity of state practice in the U.S.—reflected in the fact that some states have abolished the death penalty, while others allow a potential threshold limit of applicability as low as 10 years of age—results in very different sentences for the commission of the same crime. The deprivation by the State of an offender's life should not be made subject to the fortuitous element of where the crime took place. . . .

---

[303]Case 9647 (United States), Organization of American States, *Annual Report of the Inter-American Commission on Human Rights 1986–1987*, at 147 (1987). Another application, Case No. 10,031 (United States), filed 15 July 1987 and still pending as of the end of 1988, concerns alleged bias based on the race of the victim.

[304]The U.S. is not a party to the American Convention on Human Rights, which includes a specific prohibition against the execution of those who were under 18 or over 70 years of age at the time the crime in question was committed, but the U.S. is bound generally by the provisions of the American Declaration. *See* ORGANIZATION OF AMERICAN STATES, BASIC DOCUMENTS PERTAINING TO HUMAN RIGHTS IN THE INTER-AMERICAN SYSTEM (1988) at 1–15; Buergenthal, *The Inter-American System for the Protection of Human Rights*, in ORGANIZATION OF AMERICAN STATES, ANUARIO JURIDICO INTERAMERICANO 1981 (1982); Norris, *The Individual Petition Procedure of the Inter-American System for the Protection of Human Rights*, in Hannum, *supra* note 261, at 108–32.

[305]*Supra* note 303, at 172.

> For the federal Government of the United States to leave the issue of the application of the death penalty to juveniles to the discretion of state officials results in a patchwork scheme of legislation which makes the severity of the punishment dependent, not, primarily, on the nature of the crime committed, but on the location where it was committed. Ceding to state legislatures the determination of whether a juvenile may be executed is not of the same category as granting states the discretion to determine the age of majority for purposes of purchasing alcoholic beverages or consenting to matrimony. The failure of the federal government to preempt the states as regards this most fundamental right – the right to life – results in a pattern of legislative arbitrariness throughout the United States which results in the arbitrary deprivation of life and inequality before the law, contrary to . . . the American Declaration. . . . [306]

In June 1988, four justices of the U.S. Supreme Court held that the execution of persons who were under sixteen years old at the time of their offense violated the Eighth Amendment, citing, *inter alia*, the international consensus which exists against executing juvenile defenders.[307] Justice O'Connor joined in reversing imposition of the death penalty on the facts of the case but did not agree with the plurality's conclusion that those under sixteen at the time of their offense could never be executed.[308] Rather, she concluded only that such juveniles cannot be executed under statutes (like Oklahoma's) which do not specify a minimum age for the death penalty.[309]

---

[306]*Id.* at 172–73. The decision was adopted by a vote of 5 to 1; the dissent disagreed with the Commission's interpretation of the Declaration in light of contemporary standards and also rejected the argument that juvenile executions were prohibited by either customary international law or *jus cogens*.

This finding – essentially that federalism cannot excuse a failure by the national government to protect fundamental rights – might be compared with the situation which prevailed after the judgment of the European Court of Human Rights in Tyrer v. U.K., *supra* note 225. Despite the Court's conclusion in *Tyrer* that the practice of birching in the Isle of Man violated article 3 of the Convention, the British government refused, on grounds of domestic political practice rather than clear constitutional prohibitions, to interfere with Manx laws.

[307]Thompson v. Oklahoma, 108 S.Ct. 2687 (1988).

[308]*Id.* at 2706–11. O'Connor nevertheless cites "three major human rights treaties" which prohibit juvenile executions: the Geneva Convention Relative to the Protection of Civilian Persons in Time of War, *opened for signature* 12 Aug. 1949, *entered into force* 21 Oct. 1950, 6 U.S.T. 3516, T.I.A.S. No. 3365, 75 U.N.T.S. 287 (*entered into force* for U.S. 2 Feb. 1956), the Covenant on Civil and Political Rights, *supra* note 74, and the American Convention on Human Rights, *supra* note 84. *Id.* at 2707–08.

[309]The court granted certiorari in two other cases, to be decided during the October 1988 term, which present the issue of juvenile executions more directly. See Wilkins v. Missouri, 736 F.2d 409 (Mo. 1987), *cert. granted*, 109 S.Ct. 216 (1988), and Stanford v. Kentucky, 734 S.W.2d 781 (1987), *cert. granted*, 109 S.Ct. 217 (1988), *modified*, 109 S.Ct. 256 (1988).

FAIR TRIAL

The basic international legal norm regarding criminal law and procedure is that every accused has the right to "a fair and public hearing by a competent, independent and impartial tribunal."[310] International instruments then generally go on to guarantee certain specific additional rights of the accused,[311] such as the presumption of innocence,[312] the right to counsel (including appointed counsel, if necessary),[313] freedom from self-incrimination,[314] the right to the assistance of a translator or interpreter,[315] the right to examine witnesses,[316] the guarantee of trial within a reasonable time,[317] and the right to appeal a conviction and/or sentence.[318] These are minimum guarantees; an international tribunal must still evaluate the overall fairness of a trial, even where all of the specific rights of an accused have been respected.[319] Such an evaluation often involves consid-

---

[310]CivPol, art. 14(1). Similar wording is found in American, art. 8(1) (right to a hearing "with due guarantees"); European, art. 6(1); and African, art. 7(1)(d) (without specific mention of "fairness"). It might be noted that this right to a fair trial also extends to the determination of private rights and obligations ("in a suit at law" under CivPol; the determination of "civil" rights under European); this distinction between private and public rights stems from Roman law and has been the subject of many decisions, particularly under the European system, not relevant for present purposes. *See* 2 STRASBOURG DIGEST at 96–193; SIEGHART, *supra* note 161, at 276–78.

[311]The African Charter of Human and People's Rights merely guarantees "the right to defence," identifying only the presumption of innocence and the right to counsel as specific protections within this general right. African, art. 7(1)(c).

[312]CivPol, art. 14(2); American, art. 8(2); European, art. 6(2); African, art. 7(1)(b).

[313]CivPol, art. 14(3)(b) & (d); American, art. 8(2)(d); European, art. 6(3)(c); African, art. 7(1)(c).

[314]CivPol, art. 14(3)(g); American, art. 8(2)(g).

[315]CivPol, art. 14(2)(f); American, art. 8(2)(a); European, art. 6(3)(e).

[316]CivPol, art. 14(3)(e); American, art. 8(2)(f); European, art. 6(3)(d).

[317]CivPol, art. 14(3)(c); American, art. 8(1); European, art. 6(1); African, art. 7(1)(d).

[318]CivPol, art. 14(5); American, art. 8(2)(h).

[319]*See, e.g.*, Barberá, Messegué & Jabardo v. Spain, Eur. Court H.R., *infra* note 379; De Weer v. Belgium, App. No. 6903/75, Eur. Court H.R., Judgment of 27 Feb. 1980, Ser. A No. 35; Nielsen v. Denmark, Eur. Comm. H.R., Report of 15 Mar. 1961, 4 Y.B. EUR. CONV. ON HUMAN RIGHTS 494 (1961); Human Rights Committee, General Comment 13 (21) (article 14), *Report of the Human Rights Committee*, *supra* note 277, at 143, 144.

eration of what has been termed "equality of arms," i.e., fundamental procedural equality between the prosecution and the defense.[320]

One essential difference to be borne in mind in analyzing international norms is that between the adversarial system of justice found in the United States and other common law jurisdictions and the inquisitorial or investigative system prevalent in civil law systems. In the latter, a professional judge directs the investigation and trial proceedings; while a state prosecutor and defense attorney are present during the trial, their role is much less significant than it is during an Anglo-American trial.[321]

This difference is particularly significant with respect to rules of evidence, as an examining or investigating judge has much greater latitude to consider hearsay and other relevant facts that would be inadmissible in the adversary system. In Belgium, for example, an investigating judge is charged with assembling evidence and establishing any proof against an accused, as well as circumstances that may tend to exculpate the accused. The judge may "take any steps which are not forbidden by law or incompatible with the standing of his office," including, *inter alia*, summoning and questioning the accused; issuing a warrant for the accused's arrest or detention; hearing witnesses and confronting witnesses with each other; visiting the scene of the crime or visiting and searching any other premises; and taking possession of evidence. The case-file completed by the judge is then transmitted to the public prosecutor for comment and finally to another judge, who decides whether to discharge the accused, order the accused to stand trial, or forward the dossier to the State prosecutor.[322]

Those educated in the common law naturally believe that the opposing goals of interested parties in an adversarial system are more likely to enable the trier of fact to discover the truth, but this opinion is not unanimous.

> We proclaim to each other and to the world that the clash of adversaries is a powerful means for hammering out the truth. . . . Despite our untested statements of self-congratulation, we

---

[320] *See infra* at 92–96.

[321] *See generally, e.g.*, M. GLENDON, M. GORDON, AND C. OSAKWE, COMPARATIVE LEGAL TRADITIONS (1985); J. LANGBEIN, COMPARATIVE CRIMINAL PROCEDURE: GERMANY 61–86 (1977); J.H. MERRYMAN, THE CIVIL LAW TRADITION (1969); Pugh, *Administration of Criminal Justice in France: An Introductory Analysis*, 23 LA. L. REV. 1 (1962). For a debate on somewhat similar issues in the civil context, *cf.* Allen, Köck, Riechenberg, & Rosen, *The German Advantage in Civil Procedure: A Plea for More Details and Fewer Generalities in Comparative Scholarship*, 82 NORTHWESTERN U. L. REV. 705 (1988); Langbein, *Trashing The German Advantage*, *id.* at 763; Allen, *Idealization and Caricature in Comparative Scholarship*, *id.* at 785; Langbein, *The German Advantage in Civil Procedure*, 52 U. CHI. L. REV. 823 (1985).

[322] Summary taken from De Cubber v. Belgium, App. No. 9186/80, Eur. Court H.R., Judgment of 26 Oct. 1984, at paras. 15–18.

know that others searching after facts —in history, geography, medicine, whatever—do not emulate our adversary system. We know that most countries of the world seek justice by different routes. What is much more to the point, we know that many of the rules and devices of adversary litigation as we conduct it are not geared for, but are often aptly suited to defeat, the development of the truth.[323]

Lay judges often participate in criminal proceedings under the civil law or inquisitorial system, but neither that system nor international norms guarantee the right to trial by jury. Most countries in the world do not use jury trials, but the U.S. Supreme Court has held that juries are "necessary *to an Anglo-American regime* of ordered liberty"[324] and therefore are required in state criminal prosecutions, in addition to being required in federal prosecutions through Article III and the Sixth Amendment of the U.S. Constitution.[325] Of course, a defendant may knowingly waive his or her right to a jury trial, and, despite the theoretically fundamental role of the jury noted by the Supreme Court, jury trials are the exception rather than the rule in the United States. According to one critic, "We select, inform, control, and review juries in ways that have become ever more complicated, time-consuming, and expensive. We have made jury trial unworkable as a routine dispositive procedure, and this has led to the system of nontrial disposition that exists in well over 90 per cent of felony cases."[326]

The remainder of this section will focus on those rights guaranteed under both U.S. and international law, in particular on the emerging international requirements for a "fair trial."

Independent and Impartial Tribunal

It is fundamental that a tribunal be independent of the executive (prosecution) and of the defendant in order for a trial to be fair, and the European Court of Human Rights has defined the content of this independence in numerous cases.[327] Among the criteria it has employed to determine a tribunal's independence are the manner of appointment (al-

---

[323]Frankel, *The Search for Truth: An Umpireal View*, 123 U. PA. L.REV. 1031, 1035–37, quoted in J. LANGBEIN, *supra* note 321, at 147.

[324]Palko v. Connecticut, 302 U.S. 319, 325 (1937); emphasis added.

[325]Duncan v. Louisiana, 391 U.S. 145 (1968). There is no right to a jury trial for a petty offense, which normally is defined as an offense for which the maximum is less than six months' imprisonment. *See, e.g.*, Baldwin v. New York, 399 U.S. 117 (1970); District of Columbia v. Clawans, 300 U.S. 617 (1937). *See generally* W. LAFAVE & J. ISRAEL, *supra* note 3, at 824–53; S. SALTZBURG, *supra* note 140, at 850–909.

[326]J. LANGBEIN, *supra* note 321, at 119.

[327]*See generally* M.-A. Eissen, *Case-Law on Article 6 of the Convention* (Eur. Court H.R., 1985), at 25–28. Also *cf.* discussion of equality of arms, *infra* at 92–96.

though appointment by ministerial or government decision does not necessarily imply a lack of independence), the inclusion of judges among the tribunal's members, the length of the tribunal members' term of office, their fixed tenure in office, their independence from instructions from outside sources, and the existence of constitutional or other guarantees protecting the tribunal from outside pressures. Thus far, neither the European Court or Commission of Human Rights has found a criminal tribunal not to be independent,[328] although a lack of impartiality has been found on a few occasions. While most judges in civil law jurisdictions are professionally trained as judges, there is no requirement that a judge be legally trained under either international or U.S. law.[329]

The European Court and Commission of Human Rights have made frequent reference to the English maxim that "justice must not only be done–it must be seen to be done."[330] Thus, an "impartial" tribunal must be composed of members who not only exhibit no actual bias against an accused but who also are free from reasonable suspicion of bias because of their manner of appointment, prior dealing with the case, etc.

> Whilst impartiality normally denotes absences of prejudice or bias, its existence or otherwise can . . . be tested in various ways. A distinction can be drawn in this context between a subjective approach, that is endeavouring to ascertain the personal conviction of a given judge in a given case, and an objective approach, that is determining whether he offered guarantees sufficient to exclude any legitimate doubt in this respect. . . .
>
> In order that the courts may inspire in the public the confidence which is indispensable, account must also be taken of questions of internal organisation. If an individual, after holding in the Public Prosecutor's Department an office whose nature is such that he may have to deal with a given matter in the course of his duties, subsequently sits in the same case as a judge, the public are entitled to fear that he does not offer sufficient guarantees of impartiality.[331]

---

[328]In Sramek v. Austria, App. No. 8690/79, Eur. Court H.R., Judgment of 22 Oct. 1984, Ser. A No. 84, the court did find that an administrative tribunal was not independent or impartial, in that its rapporteur was a civil servant who was hierarchically inferior to an official appearing before the administrative tribunal.

[329]*See, e.g.*, Tumey v. Ohio, 273 U.S. 510 (1927).

[330]*See, e.g.*, Delcourt v. Belgium, App. No. 2689/65, Eur. Court H.R., Judgment of 17 Jan. 1970, Ser. A No. 11.

[331]Piersack v. Belgium, App. No. 8692/79, Eur. Court H.R., Judgment of 1 Oct. 1982, Ser. A No. 53, at paras. 30–32. While rejecting a blanket prohibition on former prosecutors serving as judges, which "would lead to an upheaval in the judicial system" of several parties to the Convention, the Court found that participation as a trial court judge by a former head of the public prosecutor's office which instituted prosecution against defendant violated the appearance of impartiality, even though there was agreement in the particular case that there was no actual bias or prejudice.

U.S. standards are similar, and the basic rule is for "a fair trial in a fair tribunal."[332] However, the European standard may be somewhat higher, perhaps because of the more active role played by the judge in the inquisitorial system. For bias to be shown in a U.S. court, a direct, personal interest in the outcome of a case often must be shown.[333]

Analogous to the "independent and impartial tribunal" requirement is the U.S. requirement that a search warrant be issued only by a "neutral and detached magistrate."[334] The Supreme Court has held that police and prosecutorial officials inherently lack the required neutrality,[335] although municipal court clerks may issue arrest warrants (and probably search warrants).[336]

In the European context, complaints frequently concern alleged confusion (and therefore anti-defendant bias) between the prosecuting and quasi-judicial functions of the *Procureur Général* or Public Prosecutor in inquisitorial systems. As in the United States, the fact that a judge was involved in prior proceedings in a case does not prevent the same judge presiding in the trial itself, even without a jury,[337] but a trial may be considered unfair if the trial judge was actively involved in an earlier investigative phase.[338]

The European Commission of Human Rights has generally rejected allegations of bias based on alleged misdirections by a judge or other

---

[332]In re Murchison, 349 U.S. 133, 136 (1965).

[333]*Compare* Tumey v. Ohio, *supra* note 329 (judge, who also served as mayor, not impartial where he received the fees and costs levied against violators) and Ward v. Monroeville, 409 U.S. 57 (1972) (judge, also mayor, not impartial where he was responsible for village finances, to which fines and costs contributed substantially) *with* Dugan v. Ohio, 277 U.S. 61 (1928) (relationship of mayor/judge who was one of five commissioners responsible for village finances too remote to warrant presumption of bias).

[334]Johnson v. U.S., 333 U.S. 10 (1948).

[335]*See* Coolidge v. New Hampshire, 440 U.S. 443 (1971).

[336]*See* Shadwick v. City of Tampa, 407 U.S. 345 (1972). Query whether search warrant cases are distinguishable from arrest warrants, in that "probable cause issues are much more complex and likely to be beyond the ken of a layman." W. LAFAVE & J. ISRAEL, *supra* note 3, at 129.

[337]*See* Withrow v. Larkin, 418 U.S. 488 (1974).

[338]*See, e.g.*, De Cubber v. Belgium, *supra* note 322 (trial by same judge who had conducted preliminary investigation unfair, despite absence of actual prejudice); Piersack v. Belgium, note 331 *supra* (violation of fair trial where presiding judge had previously acted as head of public prosecutor's department which dealt with accused's case); Delcourt v. Belgium, *supra* note 330 (Belgian Procureur Général is quasi-judicial advisor to Court of Cassation and may therefore participate in court's deliberations without presence of defense counsel); Ben Yaacoub v. Belgium, App. No. 9976/82, Eur. Comm. H.R., Report of 7 May 1985 (investigating judge's greater role in pre-trial investigation found to be incompatible with requirement of impartiality). *But compare* Hauschildt v. Denmark, App. No. 10486/83, Eur. Comm. H.R., Report of 16 July 1987 (no basis for questioning impartiality where judge's decisions on pre-trial detention are in response to requests by public prosecutor or defense counsel). *See generally* cases excerpted in 2 STRASBOURG DIGEST at 493–502.

judicial statements, although each application is examined fairly thoroughly on its merits.[339]

At least one tribunal or court within the domestic judicial system must satisfy the requirements of independence and impartiality with respect to findings of both law and facts. It is not sufficient if an appeals tribunal has jurisdiction only over legal questions, while a lower tribunal without the requisite independence or impartiality determines the facts.[340]

The degree of deference granted to national courts by European human rights organs is demonstrated in the admissibility decision of the European Commission of Human Rights involving a well-publicized trial of several alleged members of the Irish Republican Army for a bombing which killed several British servicemen.[341] The Commission first noted that the fact that the trial was conducted "in the midst of heavy security and substantial publicity" was "inevitable in a trial of this kind. . . . In itself, it cannot be a basis for holding that the trial was unfair."[342] The Commission continued:

> The Commission appreciates that the evidence adduced in connection with [one of the counts in the indictment] can be seen, retrospectively, to have been potentially prejudicial in terms of its effects on the trial of the other charges. However, it is not of the opinion that it can substitute its opinion for that of the trial judge on the question of law with which he was faced in the course of the trial, concerning the request for the severance of [that count]. The Commission's function . . . is to assess whether the proceedings in general could be considered fair. In this regard the Commission must give weight to the following factors:
>
> (1) that the trial judge, anticipating the harmful effect of introducing and then withdrawing damaging evidence, directed the jury in unambiguous terms to disregard it in relation to the applicant and the other co-defendant;
>
> (2) the Court of Appeal in its review of the evidence against the applicant did not consider that the outcome of the trial would have been different if [the count at issue] had not been included in the indictment;

---

[339]*See* cases excerpted in 2 STRASBOURG DIGEST 681–85.

[340]*See* Le Compte, Van Leuven & De Meyere v. Belgium, Apps. Nos. 6878 & 7238/75, Eur. Court H.R., Judgment of 18 Oct. 1982, Ser. A No. 54 (in the context of a determination of "civil rights and obligations"); De Weer v. Belgium, *supra* note 319 (criminal case). *Cf.* North v. Russell, 427 U.S. 328 (1976) (upholding a two-tier state system for trying misdemeanors, with non-lawyer magistrates at the first level).

[341]X v. U.K., App. No. 7542/75, Eur. Comm. H.R., dec. on admissibility of 8 May 1978 (unpublished), *excerpts reprinted in* 2 STRASBOURG DIGEST at 688–89.

[342]*Id.* See discussion of pre-trial publicity, *infra* at 103–04.

(3) that the co-defendant on the murder charge, who must also have been subject to the same alleged prejudice, was in fact acquitted.[343]

Military tribunals which determine whether or not an accused is guilty of a criminal (as opposed to disciplinary) offence also must be independent and impartial, although the fact that military judges are appointed for a fixed term by superior officers does not necessarily negate this independence.

> [A] judge's independence does not necessarily imply that he should be appointed for life or that he should be irremovable in law, i.e. that he cannot be given other duties without his consent. But it is essential that he should enjoy a certain stability, if only for a specific period, and that he should not be subject to any authority in the performance of his duties as a judge. . . . Furthermore, even if as servicemen [judges] are subject to the authority of their hierarchical superiors in their respective units, when they sit as judges, these officers and soldiers are not answerable to anyone about the way in which they administer justice.[344]

Right to Counsel

The Sixth Amendment to the U.S. Constitution states that "in all criminal prosecutions, the accused shall enjoy the right . . . to have the assistance of counsel for his defense," but it was not until the 1930s that this right was interpreted to require the appointment of counsel for an indigent defendant. The initially limited right to counsel in certain circumstances[345] was gradually expanded to include the right to appointed counsel in all felony cases in federal courts[346] and, in the celebrated case of *Gideon v. Wainwright*,[347] to all state felony cases via the due process clause of the Fourteenth Amendment. Unlike the right to a jury trial, which does not attach to "petty offenses," the right to counsel applies to any case in which imprisonment is a possible punishment.[348]

---

[343] *Id.*

[344] Sutter v. Switzerland, Ap. No. 8209/78, Eur. Comm. H.R., dec. on admissibility of 1 Mar. 1979, 16 Dec. & Rep. 166, 173-74 (selection of the senior judge of an eight-judge Divisional Tribunal, itself appointed by the government rather than military officials, by the Senior Military Prosecutor did not interfere with the required independence and impartiality).

[345] *See* Powell v. Alabama, 287 U.S. 45 (1932).

[346] *See* Johnson v. Zerbst, 304 U.S. 458 (1938).

[347] 372 U.S. 335 (1963).

[348] *See, e.g.*, Baldasar v. Illinois, 446 U.S. 222 (1980); Scott v. Illinois, 440 U.S. 367 (1979); Argersinger v. Hamlin, 407 U.S. 25 (1972). Defense counsel also play a major institutional role in the adversary system of criminal justice; see Cloud, *Forfeiting Defense Attorneys' Fees: Applying an Institutional Role Theory to Define Constitutional Rights*, 1987 WISC. L. REV. 1 (1987).

International instruments specifically guarantee the right of all defendants to be assisted by government-appointed counsel, although the precise circumstances which give rise to this right vary. The broadest guarantee is found in the American Convention on Human Rights, which declares "the inalienable right to be assisted by counsel provided by the state, . . . if the accused does not defend himself personally or engage his own counsel. . . . "[349] Both the Covenant on Civil and Political Rights and European Convention on Human Rights guarantee court-appointed counsel only "when [or "where"] the interests of justice so require," and they provide that such assistance shall be free only when the defendant does not have sufficient means to pay for it.[350] The African Charter provides, somewhat ambiguously, that an accused has "the right to defence, including the right to be defended by counsel of his choice."[351]

Faretta v. California[352] held that the Sixth Amendment guarantees the right of an accused to self-representation, which also is guaranteed under the relevant international instruments.[353] However, the specific rights of the accused are rights of the defense and not necessarily personal to the defendant. An early decision of the European Commission on Human Rights held that the European Convention "guarantees to an accused person that the proceedings against him will not take place without an adequate representation of the case for the defence, but does not give an accused person the right to decide himself in which way his defence should be assured."[354]

A defense lawyer's determination that a particular procedure was adequate may be binding upon the defendant,[355] although the European Commission has suggested that international norms may be violated if there were "a real divergence of opinion [between defendant and counsel] which could have influenced the . . . defence."[356] Imposition of a court-

---

[349]American, art. 8(2)(e).

[350]CivPol, art. 14(3)(d); European, art. 6(3)(c).

[351]African, art. 7(1)(c).

[352]422 U.S. 806 (1975).

[353]CivPol, art. 14(3d); American, art. 8(2)(d); European, art. 6(3)(c).

[354]X v. Austria, App. No. 1242/61, Eur. Comm. H.R., dec. on admissibility of 24 Nov. 1962 (unpublished), *excerpts reprinted in* 1 STRASBOURG DIGEST at 819.

[355]*See* X v. Austria, App. No. 7138/75, Eur. Comm. H.R., dec. on admissibility of 5 July 1977, 9 Dec. & Rep. 50.

[356]X v. F.R.G., App. No. 7063/75, Eur. Comm. H.R., dec. on admissibility of 7 Mar. 1977 (unpublished), *excerpts reprinted in* 1 STRASBOURG DIGEST at 826. "[A]n accused person cannot require counsel to disregard basic principles of his professional duty in the presentation of his defence [by insisting that the defense should be conducted as though admittedly true incriminating statements were not true]. If such an insistence results in the accused having to conduct his own defence, any consequent 'inequality of arms' can only be attributable to his own behaviour." X v. U.K., App. No. 8386/78, Eur. Comm. H.R., dec. on admissibility of 9 Oct. 1980, 21 Dec. & Rep. 126, 129.

appointed attorney and denial of any option to engage private counsel would surely violate international norms.[357]

Other common limitations on defense counsel, e.g., requiring membership in an appropriate professional association or limiting the number of permitted counsel, also have been upheld by the European Commission.[358] In such cases, the Commission, after noting that the right to counsel is not absolute, has generally reviewed the particular circumstances of the case in order to decide whether the restriction imposed infringed upon the fundamental fairness of the proceedings.[359]

The concern with overall fairness that characterizes European jurisprudence is comparable to that which has been adopted by U.S. courts in situations which do not fall within the guarantee of the Sixth Amendment. For example, in *Gagnon v. Scarpelli*,[360] the U.S. Supreme Court found that whether or not defense counsel was required during parole or probation revocation hearings depended on the circumstances of each case; counsel "presumptively" should be provided where the individual denies committing the alleged violation or relies upon contentions which are complex or difficult to present.

Similarly, international bodies examine the particular facts before them to see whether "the interests of justice" require the appointment of counsel. Where the legal and factual issues are simple or the offense minor, failure to provide court-appointed counsel has been found not to violate the European Convention or the Covenant on Civil and Political Rights.[361] This reasoning is analogous to that employed by the Supreme

---

[357]*See, e.g.*, Viana Acosta v. Uruguay, Comm. No. 110/1981, *Report of the Human Rights Committee*, *supra* note 277, at 169; Lopez Burgos v. Uruguay, Comm. No. 52/1979, *Report of the Human Rights Committee*, 36 UN GAOR, Supp. (No. 40) at 176 (1981).

[358]It might be noted that, at least under the European Convention, there is no right to enter the legal profession, although withdrawal or suspension of the right to practice law may fall within the requirement of a "fair trial" in the determination of "civil rights". *See* cases excerpted in 2 STRASBOURG DIGEST at 154–57; *cf.* König v. F.R.G., App. No. 6232/73, Eur. Court H.R., Judgment of 28 June 1978, Ser. A No. 27 (right to practice medicine).

[359]*See, e.g.*, X v. F.R.G., App. No. 722/60, Eur. Comm. H.R., dec. on admissibility of 6 Mar. 1962, 5 Y.B. EUR. CONV. ON HUMAN RIGHTS 104, (regulations concerning the appearance of lawyers before the courts upheld); Ensslin, Baader & Raspe v. F.R.G., *supra* note 268 (exclusion of lawyers suspected of "supporting the criminal association of the accused" and who were themselves the subject of criminal proceedings upheld, where defendants still represented by an average of 10 defense counsel); X v. U.K., App. No. 8295/78, Eur. Comm. H.R., dec. on admissibility of 9 Oct. 1978, 15 Dec. & Rep. 242 (exclusion of defendant's son as defense counsel upheld, where there was no attempt to obtain other representation and transcript "does not disclose any disadvantage to the defence or unfairness"). *Compare* Wheat v. U.S., 108 S.Ct. 1692 (1988) (upholding discretion of trial court judge to refuse defendant's counsel of choice where there is a "serious potential for conflict" of interest).

[360]411 U.S. 778, 790 (1973).

[361]*See, e.g.*, X v. F.R.G., App. No. 7300/75, Eur. Comm. H.R., dec. on admissibility of 13 Dec. 1976 (unpublished), *excerpts reprinted in* 1 STRASBOURG DIGEST at 857 ("no complex question of law or of fact"); X v. Norway, App. No. 8202/78, Eur. Comm. H.R., dec. on admissibility of 7 May 1979 (unpublished), *excerpts reprinted in id.* (minor offense); O.F. v. Norway, Comm. No. 158/1983, *Report of the Human Rights Committee*, *supra* note 278, at 204 (minor traffic offense).

Court in the latter's restriction of the right to appointed counsel to those cases in which imprisonment is a possibility,[362] although international bodies have not adopted such a definitive distinction between imprisonment and non-imprisonment cases.

The European Commission of Human Rights has found that counsel has a right to participate in an oral hearing on appeal, where such an oral hearing was unusual and the prosecuting attorney was permitted to participate.[363] Where neither the prosecution nor defense is entitled to appear at an oral hearing on appeal, the right to appointed counsel is not violated even if the appeal court has the power to order a further period of imprisonment (in the form of loss of credit for time already served) as a means of deterring frivolous appeals.[364]

> Article 6 [of the European Convention on Human Rights] required that [the applicants] be provided, in some appropriate way, with a fair procedure enabling them adequately and effectively to present their case against the possible exercise to their detriment of the power [to extend the period of their imprisonment]. . . . The interests of justice cannot, however, be taken to require an automatic grant of legal aid whenever a convicted person, with no objective likelihood of success, wishes to appeal after having received a fair trial at first instance. . . . [365]

The obligation of the state does not end with the mere appointment of counsel; it must also ensure that the right to counsel is effectively enjoyed by the accused. "A positive obligation is laid on the State to establish a system of legal assistance. The judicial authorities are not relieved of their responsibilities as soon as a lawyer has been appointed."[366] Thus, the European Court of Human Rights found a violation of the European Convention where the government failed to replace an appointed lawyer who was unable to represent an accused on appeal: "[T]he Convention is intended to guarantee not rights that are theoretical or

---

[362]*See* note 348 *supra*.

[363]Pakelli v. F.R.G., App. No. 8398/78, Eur. Comm. H.R., Report of 12 Dec. 1981.

[364]*See* Monnell & Morris v. U.K., Apps. Nos. 9562/81 & 9818/82, Eur. Court H.R., Judgment of 2 Mar. 1987, Ser. A No. 115. A chamber of 7 members of the Court overruled, by a vote of 5 to 2, the contrary conclusion of the European Commission of Human Rights that there had been a violation of the Convention.

[365]*Id*. at para. 67. Compare Douglas v. California, 372 U.S. 353 (1963), in which the Supreme Court invalidated on equal protection grounds the practice of a state appellate court of refusing to appoint counsel where it deemed such an appointment "of no value to either the defendant or the court." Appointed counsel is not required for higher discretionary appeals, Ross v. Moffitt, 417 U.S. 600 (1974), although counsel for an indigent appellant may be refused permission to withdraw from an appeal unless the appellate court finds that the appeal is "wholly frivolous." Anders v. California, 386 U.S. 738 (1967).

[366]Artico v. Italy, App. No. 6694/74, Eur. Comm. H.R., Report of 8 Mar. 1979, at para. 89.

illusory but rights that are practical and effective; this is particularly so of the rights of the defence in view of the prominent place held in a democratic society by the right to a fair trial."[367] The Human Rights Committee has declared, "The accused or his lawyer must have the right to act diligently and fearlessly in pursuing all available defences and the right to challenge the conduct of the case if they believe it to be unfair."[368]

While an accused must demonstrate in what ways the interests of justice would have been served by appointment of counsel, he or she need not demonstrate that actual prejudice resulted from lack of counsel.[369] This approach contrasts to that of the U.S. Supreme Court, which requires an accused (unless violations of the right to counsel are so extreme as to give rise to a presumption of prejudice) to "show how specific errors undermined the reliability of the finding of guilt."[370]

Presumption of Innocence

None of the international human rights texts explicitly requires that guilt be proved "beyond a reasonable doubt," which is a fundamental guarantee of U.S. due process,[371] although the Human Rights Committee has interpreted the Covenant on Civil and Political Rights as requiring the "beyond reasonable doubt" standard.[372] The European Commission of Human Rights has observed that a person can be found guilty "only on the basis of direct or indirect evidence sufficiently strong in the eyes of the law to establish . . . guilt."[373] Thus, the basic standard may simply be that guilt be established in a fair trial, before an independent and impartial tribunal. Given the presumption of innocence which *is* set forth in all the major international instruments,[374] the burden of proving guilt rests on the prosecution.

The presumption of innocence does not invalidate rebuttable infer-

---

[367]Artico v. Italy, Eur. Court H.R., Judgment of 13 May 1980, Ser. A No. 37, at para. 33; also see Goddi v. Italy, App. No. 8966/80, Eur. Court H.R., Judgment of 9 Apr. 1984, Ser. A No. 76 (appeal hearing in absence of defendant or counsel violates European Convention, where they were not responsible for failure to attend). *Cf.* Cloud, *supra* note 348.

[368]General Comment 12 (21), *Report of the Human Rights Committee, supra* note 277, at 145.

[369]*See* Artico v. Italy, *supra* note 357.

[370]U.S. v. Cronic, 466 U.S. 648 (1984); *also see* Strickland v. Washington, 466 U.S. 668 (1984) (establishing a two-pronged standard of incompetence and actual prejudice). See discussion of application of the Strickland standard to subsequent cases in J. ISRAEL AND W. LAFAVE, CRIMINAL PROCEDURE IN A NUTSHELL, CONSTITUTIONAL LIMITATIONS 379–82 (1988).

[371]*See, e.g.*, Jackson v. Virginia, 443 U.S. 307 (1979); Taylor v. Kentucky, 436 U.S. 478 (1978); In re Winship, 397 U.S. 358 (1970). However, a trial judge need not instruct the jury as to the presumption of innocence in every case. Kentucky v. Whorton, 441 U.S. 786 (1979).

[372]Human Rights Committee, General Comment 13 (21) (article 14), *Report of the Human Rights Committee, supra* note 277, at 143, 144.

[373]Austria v. Italy, App. No. 788/60, Eur. Comm. H.R., Report of 31 Mar. 1963, at para. 179.

[374]CivPol, art. 14(2); American, art. 8(2); European, art. 6(2); African, art. 7(1)(b).

ences which, if certain facts are proved, may lead to a finding of guilt. "Presumptions of fact or of law operate in every legal system. Clearly, the [European] Convention does not prohibit such presumptions in principle. It does, however, require the Contracting States to remain within certain limits in this respect as regards criminal law."[375] Even more broadly, the European Commission has upheld a conviction "on the basis of a series of circumstances, indications and inferences which together constituted presumptions capable of being regarded as evidence by the law," noting that "the validity of the [domestic] court's inferences of fact are not subject to the Commission's control."[376] The Inter-American Commission on Human Rights has stated that proving guilt by circumstantial evidence does not, in and of itself, violate the presumption of innocence.[377]

One of the few instances in which the European Commission of Human Rights has considered evidence to be insufficient to justify a conviction included complaints about confessions allegedly extracted through torture or other prohibited ill-treatment, the last-minute replacement of two judges by others unfamiliar with the case, the short time taken for the trial (one day), and the fact that the defendants were transferred from Barcelona to Madrid (site of the trial) only on the day of trial.[378] Emphasizing the fact that much of the evidence had not been publicly presented at the trial (although the defendants had consented to introduction of the 1,600-page investigation file) and expressing reservations about the proceedings taken as a whole, a closely divided (10-8) European Court of Human Rights similarly found a violation of the right to a fair trial.[379]

Under some European legal systems, the costs of a prosecution may be either reimbursed by the government in the event of an acquittal or discontinuance or charged to the defendant.

---

[375]Salabiaku v. France, App. No. 10519/83, Eur. Court H.R., Judgment of 7 Oct. 1988, Ser. A No. 141A, at para. 28 (upholding presumption of smuggling from the fact of possession of undeclared prohibited goods). *Also see* X v. U.K., App. No. 5124/71, Eur. Comm. H.R., dec. on admissibility of 19 July 1972, 42 Coll. Dec. 135 (upholding a rebuttable presumption that a person is knowingly living on the earnings of a prostitute, once the prosecution has proved that the defendant "lives or is habitually in the company of a prostitute or . . . [that he] exercises control, direction or influence over [her] movements in a way which shows he is aiding, abetting or compelling her prostitution").

[376]X v. Belgium, App. No. 7628/67, Eur. Comm. H.R., dec. on admissibility of 9 May 1977, 9 Dec. & Rep. 169, 174.

[377]Inter-American Commission on Human Rights, *Report on the Situation of Human Rights in the Republic of Nicaragua*, OAS Doc. OEA/Ser.L/V/II.53, doc. 25 (1981) at 91. The Commission did find, however, that the procedures employed by the Nicaraguan Special Tribunals created to judge former members of the Somocist National Guard (the context in which the issue of circumstantial evidence was addressed) violated "Nicaragua's commitments under the American Convention on Human Rights." *Id.* at 93.

[378]Barberá, Messengué & Jabardo v. Spain, Apps. Nos. 10588 & 10590/83, Eur. Comm. H.R., Report of 16 Oct. 1986.

[379]*Id.*, Eur. Court H.R., Judgment of 6 Dec. 1988, Ser. A No. 146.

> The mere fact of ordering certain court costs or prosecution costs against an accused when the proceedings are terminated neither by a conviction nor by an acquittal cannot in itself amount to a violation of the presumption of innocence. . . . On the other hand, a problem does arise under Article 6(2) if the reasons for the court's decision or any other precise and conclusive evidence show that the apportionment of these costs, as ordered, results from an appraisal of the guilt of the accused, so that the costs ordered against him may appear as a sort of penalty imposed on grounds of suspicion.[380]

Where reimbursement has been withheld on the basis of various statutory exceptions, the European Court of Human Rights has generally found no violation of the presumption of innocence where the court order denying reimbursement referred only to a "state of suspicion" against the accused rather than presuming guilt.[381] Similarly, termination of minor proceedings under the Austrian Penal Code based on a "state of suspicion" rather than a finding of guilt have been held not to violate the presumption of innocence guaranteed in article 6(2) of the European Convention.[382]

The presumption of innocence extends not only to situations where criminal charges have been brought but prohibits public authorities from declaring a person guilty of an offense prior to conviction by a competent court.[383] The European Commission and Court have considered several allegations of improper public statements by government officials or alleged prejudice on the part of trial court judges; however, it does not

---

[380]Minelli v. Switzerland, App. No. 8660/79, Eur. Comm. H.R., Report of 6 May 1981, 21 Dec. & Rep. 199, at para 31.

[381]*See, e.g.*, Lutz v. F.R.G., App. No. 9912/82, App. No. 9912/82, Eur. Court H.R., Judgment of 25 Aug. 1987, Ser. A No. 123 (statement by the German court that, had the prosecution not been barred by statute, the defendant "would almost certainly have been found guilty of an offence"); Englert v. F.R.G., App. No. 10282/83, *id.* (statement by the domestic court that "the circumstances rebutting the presumption of innocence are . . . so overwhelming that a conviction is clearly more likely than an acquittal"); Nölkenbockhoff v. F.R.G., App. No. 10300/83, *id.* (conviction at trial court was sufficient reason to deny reimbursement for costs, where defendant died during appeal process). The European Commission of Human Rights had found a violation of the Convention in all three cases.

In an earlier case, where prosecution was barred by a statute of limitations, the Court held that requiring an accused to pay for the costs of a private prosecution as well as his own costs did imply guilt and therefore violated the presumption of innocence. Minelli v. Switzerland, App. No. 8660/79, Eur. Court H.R., Judgment of 15 Mar. 1983, Ser. A No. 62. *Also see* I & C v. Switzerland, App. No. 10107/82, Eur. Comm. H.R., dec. on admissibility of 4 Dec. 1985 (violation found where prosecution barred by statute of limitations, but domestic court nevertheless charged some investigation and court costs to the accused, while observing that defendants "repeatedly grossly contravened" applicable statutes and "after all committed the offenses").

[382]Adolf v. Austria, App. No. 8269/78, Eur. Court H.R., Judgment of 26 Mar. 1982, Ser. A No. 49, *rev'g* Eur. Comm. H.R., Report of 8 Oct. 1980 (holding that the challenged Austrian statute, as applied, implied a finding of guilt).

[383]*See, e.g.*, X v. Austria, App. No. 9077/80, Eur. Comm. H.R., dec. on admissibility of 6 Oct. 1981, 26 Dec. & Rep. 211; Krause v. Switzerland, App. No. 7986/77, Eur. Comm. H.R., dec. on admissibility of 3 Oct. 1978, 21 Y.B. Eur. Conv. on Human Rights 516.

appear that either has yet concluded that such allegations were well-founded in the particular circumstances.[384] Unlike the situation in the United States, reference to a defendant's prior convictions is not regarded as incompatible with the guarantees of a fair trial and the presumption of innocence under the European Convention.[385]

"Equality of Arms" Between Prosecution and Defense

Under the inquisitorial system, the investigating judge marshals evidence both for and against the accused; there is thus little need for either prosecution or defense in the subsequent trial to request disclosure or discovery of information gathered by the other side.[386] Under traditional common law norms, a defendant enjoyed no general or inherent right to discovery, and the U.S. Supreme Court has noted that there is no general constitutional right to discovery.[387]

Nevertheless, due process has been held to require, in some circumstances, the disclosure to the defense of exculpatory evidence in the possession of the prosecution.[388] The concern with the fundamental fairness of a trial is reflected in the rule set forth in *United States v. Agurs*,[389] in which the Supreme Court held that a conviction should only be overturned when the evidence withheld had a material effect in the eyes of the trial judge, i.e., whether the concealed evidence created a reasonable doubt that would not have existed at the trial. In *United States v. Bagley*,[390] the Court rephrased the *Agurs* test to resemble the scrutiny given to claims of ineffective assistance of counsel, holding that the "standard of materiality" is whether there is a reasonable probability that withholding the requested information affected the outcome of the trial.

U.S. courts also have recognized "a trial court's discretionary authority to require pretrial discovery as an exercise of its inherent powers to

---

[384]*Cf., e.g.*, X v. Netherlands, App. No. 8361/78, Eur. Comm. H.R., dec. on admissibility of 17 Dec. 1981, 27 Dec. & Rep. 37; Krause v. Switzerland, *supra* note 383; cases excerpted in 2 STRASBOURG DIGEST at 728–38.

[385]*See, e.g.*, X v. Denmark, App. No. 2518/65, Eur. Comm. H.R., dec. on admissibility of 14 Dec. 1965, 7 Y.B. EUR. CONV. ON HUMAN RIGHTS 370 (noting that information as to prior convictions is commonly given during the trial in a number of European countries), and cases excerpted in 2 STRASBOURG DIGEST at 738–40.

[386]*But see* Lamy v. Belgium, *supra* note 148 (defense counsel must be granted access to examining judge's and police files in order to challenge detention on remand).

[387]Weatherford v. Bursey, 429 U.S. 545 (1977).

[388]*See* U.S. v. Bagley, 473 U.S. 667 (1985); U.S. v. Agurs, 427 U.S. 97 (1976); Brady v. Maryland, 373 U.S. 83 (1963); Mooney v. Holohan, 294 U.S. 103 (1935). *See generally* LAFAVE & ISRAEL, *supra* note 3, at 753–64

[389] Note 388 *supra*. *Agurs* did not involve a specific request by the defendant for the information not disclosed by the prosecution.

[390]Note 388 *supra*. *Cf.* Case Note, *Bagley v. United States: Specific Requests and the Prosecutorial Duty to Disclose Evidence*, 1986 DUKE L.J. 892 (1986).

control the trial process."[391] Discovery in the criminal context is largely regulated by state and federal statutes, e.g., the Federal Rules of Criminal Procedure. The Rules allow a defendant access to prior statements of the defendant; the defendant's prior criminal record; documents and tangible objects; and reports of examinations and texts.[392] However, the defendant's right to the limited access set forth in the Rules is not absolute. In *United States v. Pelton*,[393] for example, the defendant was denied access to a tape of his own conversations because of concern over harassment of or possible danger to the government's other witnesses. As a general rule, the government's witnesses do not have to talk to the defendant or the defendant's lawyers.

In a related area, there is no duty on the prosecution to preserve evidence which might be of use to defense, absent bad faith.[394] However, where the prosecution knowingly fails to correct false evidence, any resulting conviction may be overturned.[395]

The concept of "equality of arms" comprises other questions of procedural inequality which would compromise the fundamental fairness of the proceedings. For example, the European Court of Human Rights found a violation of procedural equality where an expert witness for the prosecution was granted far wider rights to participate in the trial—including attendance throughout the hearings and the possibility of questioning witnesses and the accused—than an expert witness called by the defence.[396] While, under the relevant law, the expert was considered "a neutral and impartial auxiliary of the court" and was appointed by the domestic court itself, the European Court considered that there was reason for doubting the expert's neutrality when the prosecution had been brought on the basis of a report prepared by that same expert.[397]

---

[391]W. LaFave & J. Israel, *supra* note 3, at 730. For a discussion of the various theories of discovery, see *id*. at 725–30.

[392]Fed. R. Crim. Pro. 16. Compare, *e.g.*, Jespers v. Belgium, App. No. 8403/78, Eur. Comm. H.R., Report of 14 Dec. 1981, 27 Dec. & Rep. 61 (no violation of the principle of "equality of arms" where prosecution refused to disclose contents of "special folder" to defendant, absent evidence that material documents were included in the file).

[393]578 F.2d 701, 706–08 (8th Cir. 1978).

[394]Arizona v. Youngblood, 57 U.S.L.W. 4013 (29 Nov. 1988) (failure to preserve possibly useful evidence of sexual assault).

[395]*See* Giglio v. U.S. 405 U.S. 150 (1972) (failure to correct inaccurate testimony regarding prosecution promise to witness, even though particular government attorney did not have actual knowledge of inaccuracy); Napue v. Illinois, 360 U.S. 264 (1959) (knowing failure to correct testimony); Alcorta v. Texas, 355 U.S. 28 (1957) (reversing a conviction where the prosecutor knowingly allowed a witness to create a false impression at trial); Mooney v. Holohan, *supra* note 388 (conviction based solely on testimony which the prosecutor knew to be perjured).

While the European Commission and Court of Human Rights will not necessarily find a violation of procedural equality where neither the defendant nor the prosecution is allowed to present oral arguments on appeal,[398] such a right was found to be essential when an appellate court is called upon to examine both the facts and the law.[399] At the trial court level, the defense should have the opportunity to confront directly all adverse witnesses.[400]

The right to compulsory process found in the Sixth Amendment to the U.S. Constitution may be somewhat narrower under international standards, although there have been few decided cases. For example, the American Convention on Human Rights provides that a defendant has the right "to obtain the appearance, as witnesses, of experts or other persons *who may throw light on the facts*."[401] Under the Covenant on Civil and Political Rights and the European Convention, a defendant may "obtain the attendance and examination of witnesses on his behalf *under the same conditions as witnesses against him*."[402] This "does not imply the right to have witnesses called without restriction. . . . [nor does it mean] that municipal law cannot lay down conditions for the admission and examination of witnesses, provided that such conditions are identical for witnesses on both sides. Similarly, the competent judicial authorities . . . are free . . . to decide whether the hearing of a witness for the defence is likely to assist in ascertaining the truth, and if not, to refuse to call that witness."[403]

---

[396] Bönisch v. Austria, App. No. 8658/79, Eur. Court H.R., Judgment of 6 May 1985, Ser. A No. 92.

[397] *Id.* at paras. 31–32.

[398] *See, e.g.*, X v. U.K., App. No. 5871/72, Eur. Comm. H.R., dec. on admissibility of 30 Sept. 1974, 1 Dec. & Rep. 54; X v. F.R.G., App. No. 3139/67, Eur. Comm. H.R., dec. on admissibility of 6 Feb. 1968, 26 Coll. Dec. 77; X v. Austria, App. No. 2243/64, Eur. Comm. H.R., dec. on admissibility of 16 July 1965, 17 Coll. Dec. 22.

[399] Ekbatani v. Sweden, App. No. 10563/83, Eur. Court H.R., Judgment of 26 May 1988, Ser. A No. 134.

[400] *See* Bricmont v. Belgium, App. No. 10857/84, Eur. Comm. H.R., Report of 15 Oct. 1987 (defendants had right to confront Prince Charles, Count of Flanders, former Regent of the Kingdom of Belgium, who instituted criminal proceedings against them); *cf.* Barberá, Messengué & Jabardo v. Spain, *supra* note 379. Hearsay evidence from anonymous informers may, however, be admitted without necessarily violating the Convention. *See* cases cited *infra* note 413.

[401] American, art. 8(2)(f) (emphasis added).

[402] CivPol, art. 14(3)(e); European, art. 6(3)(d) (emphasis added).

[403] Austria v. Italy, *supra* note 373, at 772; other cases are cited in 2 STRASBOURG DIGEST 881–99. President Carter interpreted the comparable provisions of CivPol and American to permit requiring an indigent defendant to show that a requested witness is necessary in order for attendance of that witness to be compelled by the court. Message of the President, *supra* note 20, at xiii, xix (consistent with Fed.R.Crim.P. 17, which provides that a subpoena is to be issued where the "presence of the witness is necessary to an adequate defense"). "[T]he word 'necessary' has been construed to mean only relevant, material, and useful to an adequate defense." W. LAFAVE & J. ISRAEL, *supra* note 3, at 878.

The Covenant on Civil and Political Rights specifically provides that everyone charged with a criminal offense has the right to be tried "in his presence,"[404] and such a right is implicit in other international instruments. However, the Human Rights Committee has observed that trials *in absentia* are not invariably impermissible "irrespective of the reasons for the accused person's absence. Indeed, proceedings *in absentia* are in some circumstances (for instance, when the accused person, although informed of the proceedings sufficiently in advance, declines to exercise his right to be present) permissible in the interest of the proper administration of justice. . . . Judgment *in absentia* requires that, notwithstanding the absence of the accused, all due notification has been made to inform him of the date and place of his trial and to request his attendance."[405] Where the prosecution had taken inadequate steps to contact the accused and he did not, in fact, have any knowledge of the pending criminal proceedings, conduct of a trial in the defendant's absence (even though court-appointed counsel was present), can violate the requirements of a fair trial.[406]

The plea-bargaining which is an essential element of the U.S. criminal justice system is rare in civil law countries.[407] In one of the few cases to address the issue indirectly, the European Court of Human Rights held that pressure brought on an accused to pay a relatively small fine rather than face the much more serious alternative of closure of his business violated the right to a fair trial, although such a waiver of trial through payment of a fine was not held, in principle, to violate the Convention.[408]

In the United States, on the other hand, plea bargaining is the norm and has been repeatedly upheld by the Supreme Court.[409] A prosecutor

---

[404]CivPol, art. 14(3)(d).

[405]Mbenge v. Zaire, Comm. No. 16/1977, *Report of the Human Rights Committee*, *supra* note 248, at 134, 138.

[406]*See* Colozza v. Italy, App. No. 9024/80, Eur. Court H.R., Judgment of 12 Feb. 1985, Ser. A No. 39. In the United States, a defendant's right to be present at trial has both a due process and Sixth Amendment component and includes the right to be present at all trial-related proceedings in which there is a reasonably substantial relationship between the defendant's presence and his or her opportunity to present a full defense. *See* Stincer v. Kentucky, 107 S.Ct. 2658 (1987); U.S. v. Gagnon, 470 U.S. 522 (1985); Illinois v. Allen, 397 U.S. 337 (1970).

[407]*See* W. LAFAVE & J. ISRAEL, *supra* note 3, at 766–72, for a summary of the major arguments for and against plea bargaining.

[408]De Weer v. Belgium, note 319 *supra*. The Court did not address the separate issue of whether such pressures – which have obvious similarities to the plea-bargaining common in U.S. jurisdictions – also violated the presumption of innocence, although the European Commission had found that provisional closure of the shop during the preliminary investigation, taken in isolation from the alleged constraint placed on the accused to pay a fine, would not violate the presumption of innocence. *Id.*, Eur. Comm. H.R., Report of 5 Oct. 1978, at paras. 60–64.

[409]*See, e.g.*, Corbitt v. New Jersey, 439 U.S. 212 (1978); Bordenkircher v. Hayes, 434 U.S. 357 (1978); Santobello v. New York, 404 U.S. 257 (1971).

may charge and convict a defendant as a habitual criminal, subject to a mandatory life sentence, because the defendant refused to plead guilty to a lesser charge subject to a much lighter sentence.[410] However, the judge accepting any plea of guilty must ensure that the plea is knowing and voluntary,[411] and the prosecution must keep any bargain it makes with the defendant.[412]

Standards of Evidence

The exclusion of improperly obtained evidence is not generally required under the investigative-inquisitorial system of criminal justice or international norms. Nevertheless, the requirements of a fair trial may lead to the conclusion that the use of certain evidence has interfered with the rights of the defense or the presumption of innocence and thus is impermissible under the more general international standards of due process.

The European Commission and Court of Human Rights have considered these questions on a case-by-case basis, in effect adopting a standard of harmless error and rarely finding a violation of the right to a fair trial if sufficient evidence of an accused's guilt exists in addition to that which is being challenged. Thus, the admission of hearsay,[413] evidence allegedly planted by the police,[414] surprise evidence,[415] or incriminating statements made during a police investigation,[416] have been held not to violate the right to a fair trial. There was also no violation found where relevant evidence in the possession of the prosecution was lost[417] or in a case where a private prosecutor (private prosecutions are permitted

---

[410]Bordenkircher v. Hayes, *supra* note 409.

[411]Boykin v. Alabama, 395 U.S. 238 (1969).

[412]Santobello v. New York, *supra* note 409.

[413]*See, e.g.,* X v. Belgium, App. No. 8417/78, Eur. Comm. H.R., dec. on admissibility of 7 May 1979, 19 Dec. & Rep. 200; X v. F.R.G., App. No. 8414/78, Eur. Comm. H.R., dec. on admissibility of 4 July 1979, 17 Dec. & Rep. 231; X v. Austria, App. No. 4428/70, Eur. Comm. H.R., dec. on admissibility of 1 June 1972, 15 Y.B. EUR. CONV. ON HUMAN RIGHTS 264. However, the Commission recently found unanimously that a conviction based exclusively on hearsay declarations by two anonymous witnesses violated the defendant's right to a fair trial. Kostovski v. Netherlands, App. No. 11454/85, Eur. Comm. H.R., Report of 12 May 1988.

[414]*See* X v. U.K., App. No. 5327/71, Eur. Comm. H.R., dec. on admissibility of 14 Dec. 1972, 43 Coll. Dec. 85.

[415]*See* X v. U.K., App. No. 5282/71, Eur. Comm. H.R., dec. on admissibility of 12 July 1972, 42 Coll. Dec. 99.

[416]*See* X v. F.R.G., App. No. 4483/70, Eur. Comm. H.R., dec. on admissibility of 12 July 1971, 38 Coll. Dec. 77.

[417]*See* X v. F.R.G., App. No. 8770/79, Eur. Comm. H.R., dec. on admissibility of 10 July 1981 (unpublished), *excerpts reprinted in* 2 STRASBOURG DIGEST 405; compare Arizona v. Youngblood, *supra* note 394.

under many continental legal systems) refused, based on parliamentary immunity, to testify in a criminal defamation case.[418]

The issue of the exclusion of an illegally obtained recording of a telephone conversation was squarely presented to the European Commission of Human Rights in *Schenk v. Switzerland*.[419] In *Schenk*, the applicant was convicted of attempted incitement to murder, based largely on a secret recording of telephone conversations made by the person employed to commit the murder. While the recording, to which one of the parties obviously had consented, might not have been unlawful under the laws of other countries, it was agreed that the making of the recording was illegal under Swiss law. Neither the police nor any other public authorities were involved in making the recording, which was admitted into evidence by the Swiss courts.

The Commission first underscored the limited supervisory role it exercises in evidentiary matters.

> The Commission notes first that . . . its only task is to ensure the observance of the obligations undertaken by the parties to the Convention. In particular, it is not competent to deal with an application alleging that errors of law or fact have been omitted [sic] by domestic courts, except where it considers that such errors might have involved a possible violation of any of the rights and freedoms set out in the Convention.
>
> The Commission points out that the assessment of evidence comes with the appreciation of independent and impartial courts and cannot be reviewed by the Commission unless there is an indication that the judge has drawn grossly unfair or arbitrary conclusions from the facts before him. . . .
>
> Although Article 6 para. 1 guarantees for everyone the right to a fair trial, "this provision does not . . . lay down rules as to the evidence as such, and in particular as to its admissibility and probative value, these questions being essentially dependent on domestic legislation". The Commission does not examine whether the Courts have correctly assessed the evidence, but whether evidence has been presented in such a manner and the proceedings in general have been conducted in such a way that the accused has had a fair trial.
>
> . . . [T]hese considerations apply particularly to proceedings in trial courts, where factors such as the circumstances in which the offence was committed, the evidence and the personality of

---

[418] *See* X v. Belgium, App. No. 8802/79, Eur. Comm. H.R., dec. on admissibility of 11 Dec. 1981 (unpublished), *excerpts reprinted in* 2 STRASBOURG DIGEST 407–08.

[419] App. No. 10862/84, Eur. Comm. H.R., Report of 14 May 1987.

the accused, are of crucial importance in determining the accused's guilt. . . .

[T]he Convention contains no express or implied requirement that evidence obtained unlawfully under domestic law should necessarily be ruled inadmissible.[420]

Looking at the specific case before it, the Commission found that the Swiss court's determination of guilt had been founded "on a number of factors distinct from the contents of the recording—such as evidence given by witnesses—all of which confirm the applicant's guilt."[421] It therefore held that, in the specific circumstances of the case, the use in evidence of the unlawful recording did not violate the guarantee of a fair trial.[422] The Court subsequently agreed with the Commission's analysis, confirming that "Article 6 of the Convention . . . does not lay down any rules on the admissibility of evidence as such, which is therefore primarily a matter for regulation under national law."[423]

One of the few cases in which evidence was found to have led to an improper conviction in violation of the European Convention is *Unterpertinger v. Austria*.[424] In *Unterpertinger*, statements given by the defendant's wife and step-daughter to the police were admitted at trial, although the wife and step-daughter refused (as they were entitled to do under applicable Austrian law) to testify at the trial. After a closely divided European Commission found no violation of the right to a fair trial, the European Court unanimously reversed that finding in rather summary fashion.

> By refusing to give evidence in court, [the defendant's wife and step-daughter] prevented the applicant from examining them or having them examined on their statements. Admittedly, he was able to submit his comments freely during the hearing, but the Court of Appeal refused to admit the evidence he sought to adduce in order to put his former wife's and step-daughter's credibility in doubt.

---

[420]*Id.* at paras. 56–59; citations omitted.

[421]*Id.* at para. 65.

[422]*See also* Scheichelbauer v. Austria, App. No. 2645/67, Eur. Comm. H.R., Report of 16 Dec. 1970, 14 Y.B. EUR. CONV. ON HUMAN RIGHTS 902 (use of recording made secretly by co-defendant of conversation with accused and introduced in former's defense did not violate right to fair trial); X v. Belgium, App. No. 8876/80, Eur. Comm. H.R., dec. on admissibility of 16 Oct. 1980, 23 Dec. & Rep. 233 (same, except recording made by police of confrontation between co-defendants).

Compare the U.S. doctrine of "harmless error" propounded in, *e.g.*, Chapman v. California, 386 U.S. 18 (1967), and subsequent cases; see generally W. LAFAVE & J. ISRAEL, *supra* note 3, at 995–1008.

[423]Schenk v. Switzerland, Eur. Court H.R., Judgment of 12 July 1988, Ser. A No. 140, at para. 46.

[424]App. No. 9120/80, Eur. Court H.R., Judgment of 24 Nov. 1986, Ser. A No. 110.

It is true that the statements made by Mrs. Unterpertinger and Miss Tappeiner [the step-daughter] were not the only evidence before the courts. . . . However, it is clear . . . that the Court of Appeal based the applicant's conviction mainly on the statements made by Mrs. Unterpertinger and Miss Tappeiner to the police. It did not treat these simply as items of information but as proof of the truth of the accusations made by the women at the time. Admittedly, it was for the Court of Appeal to assess the material before it as well as the relevance of the evidence which the accused sought to adduce; but Mr. Unterpertinger was nevertheless convicted on the basis of "testimony" in respect of which his defence rights were appreciably restricted.

That being so, the applicant did not have a fair trial. . . . [425]

Search and Seizure/Right to Privacy

The Fourth Amendment's prohibition against unreasonable searches and seizures has resulted in a massive and often arcane U.S. jurisprudence, and Fourth Amendment issues constitute a substantial part of U.S. criminal procedure case books and treatises.[426] However, as noted in the immediately preceding section, there is no international equivalent to the Fourth Amendment "exclusionary rule" against unconstitutionally obtained evidence. Nor do international human rights norms address the issue of sanctioning or deterring police practices (except indirectly through the awarding of compensation to those whose rights have been violated).

International norms directly protect the individual's right to privacy or respect for private life, which must then be balanced against larger societal interests.[427] This balance is struck either by a general prohibition against "arbitrary", "unlawful", or "abusive" interference with privacy[428] or by a detailed listing of the circumstances under which privacy rights may be restricted. The latter approach is adopted in article 8(2) of the European Convention on Human Rights, which provides that private and family life, home, and correspondence may be interfered with only as "necessary in a democratic society in the interests of national security,

---

[425]*Id.* at paras. 32-33.

[426]*See, e.g.*, W. LaFave & J. Israel, *supra* note 3, at 76-246; S. Saltzburg, *supra* note 140, at 32-379; R. Allen & R. Kuhns, Constitutional Criminal Procedure 429-764 (1985); H. Uviller, The Processes of Criminal Justice: Investigation and Adjudication 6-487 (1979); Y. Kamisar, W. LaFave & J. Israel, Modern Criminal Procedure 208-473 (6th ed. 1986); P. Johnson, Cases and Materials on Criminal Procedure 2-345 (1988).

[427]*Cf.* Human Rights Committee, General Comment 16 (32) (art. 17), *Report of the Human Rights Committee*, 43 UN GAOR, Supp. (No. 40), UN Doc. A/43/40 (1988) at 181.

[428]CivPol, art. 17(1); American, art. 112(2).

public safety or the economic well-being of the country, for the prevention of disorder or crime, for the protection of health or morals, or for the protection of the rights and freedoms of others"; in every case, the interference also must be "in accordance with the law".[429]

Except insofar as the use of illegally seized evidence may undermine the international guarantee of a fair trial—the equivalent, in many respects, of the U.S. due process standard —questions of illegal searches and seizures thus arise internationally in a civil rather than criminal context. Without entering into a broad discussion of the international right to privacy, two cases before the European Court of Human Rights which considered the sensitive issue of wiretapping by government authorities are discussed below, by way of example. Both cases arose in the context of civil suits challenging government surveillance rather than as challenges to evidence offered in a criminal trial.

Klass and others v. F.R.G.[430] upheld wiretapping of suspected terrorists, on the grounds that such interference was "necessary in a democratic society" to protect "national security" (one of the permissible restrictions under article 8(2) of the European Convention). Despite its observation that "it is in principle desirable to entrust supervisory control [over government surveillance] to a judge," the Court in *Klass* upheld a non-judicial system of secret surveillance in which oversight was exercised by executive and parliamentary authorities.[432]

Malone v. U.K.[433] held that the standards for executive-ordered wiretapping directed against suspected criminals in the United Kingdom were so uncertain and obscure that the interference could not be considered to be "in accordance with the law" as required by the Convention.[434] A concurring opinion by Judge Pettiti offered a broader view of the issues posed by governmental surveillance and outlined a principle of judicial

---

[429]Compare this listing with the test of Schmerber v. California, 384 U.S. 757 (1966), in which the extent of the intrusion on a person's privacy is balanced against the government's need for the evidence.

[430]App. No. 5029/71, Eur. Court H.R., Judgment of 6 Sept. 1978, Ser. A No. 28. Relevant excerpts from the Klass case may be found in H. HANNUM, *supra* note 100, at 107–13.

[431]Klass v. F.R.G., *supra* note 430, at para. 56.

[432]In the U.S., the Foreign Intelligence Surveillance Act of 1978, 50 U.S.C. §§ 1801–1811, provides that the President may authorize surveillance without a court order, but only if the surveillance is directed at communications between foreign powers; a warrant procedure is established for security cases involving U.S. citizens. *Cf.* U.S. v. U.S. District Court, 407 U.S. 297 (1972) (Fourth Amendment protections necessary for those suspected of "unorthodox" political beliefs).

[433]App. No. 8691/79, Eur. Court H.R., Judgment of 2 Aug. 1984, Ser A No. 82.

[434]The Court came to a similar conclusion with respect to telephone "metering", *i.e.*, monitoring of the numbers called. *Compare* Smith v. Maryland, 442 U.S. 735 (1979) (use of a "pen register" to keep a record of telephone numbers dialed is not a search).

oversight and analogies to warrant-based searches which would be familiar to American lawyers:

> The danger threatening democratic societies in the years 1980–1990 stems from the temptation facing public authorities to "see into" the life of the citizen. In order to answer the needs of planning and of social and tax policy, the State is obliged to amplify the scale of its interferences [with private life]. In its administrative systems, the State is being led to proliferate and then to computerise its personal data-files. Already in several of the member States of the Council of Europe each citizen is entered on 200 to 400 data-files.
>
> At a further stage, public authorities seek, for the purposes of their statistics and decision-making processes, to build up a "profile" of each citizen. Enquiries become more numerous; telephone tapping constitutes one of the favoured means of this permanent investigation.
>
> Telephone tapping during the last thirty years benefited from many "improvements" which have aggravated the dangers of interference in private life. The product of the interception can be stored on magnetic tapes and processed in postal or other centres equipped with the most sophisticated material. The amateurish tapping effected by police officers or post office employees now exists only as a memory of pre-war novels. The encoding of programmes and tapes, their decoding, and computer processing make it possible for interceptions to be multiplied a hundredfold and to be analysed in shorter and shorter time-spans, if need be by computer. Through use of the "mosaic" technique, a complete picture can be assembled of the life-style of even the "model" citizen. . . .
>
> Concurrently with developments in the techniques of interception, the aims pursued by the authorities have diversified. Police interception for the prevention of crime is only one of the practices employed; to this should be added political interceptions, interceptions of communications of journalists and leading figures, not to mention interceptions required by national defence and State security, which are included in the "top-secret" category and not dealt with in the Court's judgment or the present opinion.
>
> Most of the member States of the Council of Europe have felt the need to introduce legislation on the matter in order to bring to an end the abuses which were proliferating and making vulnerable even those in power.
>
> The legislative technique most often employed is that of

> criminal procedure: the interception of communications is made subject to the decision and control of a judge within the framework of a criminal investigation by means of provisions similar to those governing searches carried out on the authority of a warrant.
>
> The order by the judge must specify the circumstances justifying the measure, if need be subject to review by an appeal court. Variations exist according to the types of system and code of criminal procedure.
>
> The governing principle of these laws is the separation of executive and judicial powers, that is to say, not to confer on the executive the initiative and the control of the interception. . . .
>
> Even if a "law". . . contains detailed rules which do not merely legalise practices but define and delimit them, the lack of judicial control could still entail, in my view, a violation of Article 8 para. 2.[435]

The European Court has not yet directly addressed the issue of whether judicial oversight is required in electronic surveillance of suspected criminals (as opposed to suspected terrorists or others who threaten national security), although Pettiti's concurrence may prove to be persuasive.[436] The European Commission has found that the fact that government authorities exceed the scope of a judge-ordered wiretap does not, by itself, violate any provision of the European Convention, such as the right to privacy.[437]

Self-incrimination

Protection against self-incrimination, guaranteed under the Fifth Amendment to the U.S. Constitution, is also found in article 14(3)(g) of the Covenant on Civil and Political Rights and article 8(2)(g) of the American Convention on Human Rights, although it is not explicitly guaranteed in the European or African conventions. In fact, many foreign jurisdictions permit negative inferences to be drawn from an accused's silence, and it is not surprising that most defendants do speak in such situations.[438] Even where such an inference cannot be drawn, as is the

---

[435]Malone v. U.K., *supra* note 433, at 36–38 (provisional translation). Compare, *e.g.*, the judicial order required for electronic surveillance of criminal suspects under Title III of the Omnibus Crime Control and Safe Streets Act of 1968, 18 U.S.C. §§ 2510–2520.

[436]*Cf.* Justice Harlan's dissent in U.S. v. White, 401 U.S. 745 (1971).

[437]*See* X v. F.R.G., App. No. 8290/78, Eur. Comm. H.R., dec. on admissibility of 13 Dec. 1979, 18 Dec. & Rep. 176.

[438]*See generally* Comment, *The Accused's Privilege against Self-Incrimination in the Civil Law*, 11 AM. J. COMP. L. 585 (1962). In the U.S., any comment by the prosecution or court regarding a defendant's failure to testify is prohibited, Griffin v. California, 380 U.S. 609 (1965), and, upon defense request, the jury must be instructed to disregard a defendant's silence, Carter v. Kentucky, 450 U.S. 288 (1981).

case in the Federal Republic of Germany, a judge may still directly question the accused (who retains the right to refuse to respond).[439]

Nevertheless, other international protections – such as the presumption of innocence or the prohibition against torture and other ill-treatment – offer protections against coerced confessions or testimony. For example, the European Commission of Human Rights has suggested in dictum that the use as evidence of a confession extracted by ill-treatment could be regarded as violating the presumption of innocence, in addition to the prohibition against torture or inhuman or degrading treatment.[440] The Human Rights Committee also has referred to the protection of physical integrity in this context, recommending that "[t]he law should require that evidence provided by means of such methods [torture, etc.] or any other form of compulsion is wholly unacceptable."[441]

Physical or bodily evidence from an accused (e.g., blood samples, fingerprints, photographs) may be obtained without violating the privilege against self-incrimination or presumption of innocence, and there appear to be no substantive distinctions between international and U.S. jurisprudence on these issues.[442] It is likely that the intrusiveness which shocked the conscience of the U.S. Supreme Court in *Rochin v. California*[443] would have a similar impact on international tribunals.

Prejudicial Publicity and Public Trials

All the major international human rights instruments guarantee the right of freedom of speech and expression, but they also provide, more specifically than does the First Amendment to the U.S. Constitution, for permissible restrictions upon the right.[444] Both the Covenant on Civil and

---

[439]*See* J. LANGBEIN, ***supra*** note 321, at 65, 71–73.

[440]Austria v. Italy, ***supra*** note 373, at para. 179.

[441]Human Rights Committee, General Comment 13 (21), ***Report of the Human Rights Committee***, ***supra*** note 277, at 143, 146.

[442]*Compare, e.g.*, X v. F.R.G., App. No. 1307/61, Eur. Comm. H.R., dec. on admissibility of 4 Oct. 1962, 5 Y.B. EUR. CONV. ON HUMAN RIGHTS 230 (keeping of police records, including documents, photographs, and fingerprints); X v. Netherlands, App. No. 8239/78, Eur. Comm. H.R., dec. on admissibility of 4 Dec. 1978, 16 Dec. & Rep. 184 (blood test to determine alcohol content); X v. U.K., App. No. 5877/72, Eur. Comm. H.R., dec. on admissibility of 12 Oct. 1973, 16 Y.B. EUR. CONV. ON HUMAN RIGHTS 328 (police photographs taken during public demonstration); and X v. F.R.G., App. No. 5339/72, Eur. Comm. H.R., dec. on admissibility of 2 Apr. 1973, 43 Coll. Dec. 156 (intimate photographs introduced at trial); ***with, e.g.***, Holt v. U.S., 218 U.S. 245 (1910) (modeling clothing); Schmerber v. California, ***supra*** note 429 (blood test to determine alcohol content, distinguishing between testimonial and physical evidence); U.S. v. Wade, 388 U.S. 218 (1967) (speaking and appearing in police line-up); Gilbert v. California, 388 U.S. 263 (1967) (handwriting sample).

[443]342 U.S. 165 (1952) (forcibly inducing vomiting by stomach pump); *also see* Winston v. Lee, 470 U.S. 753 (1985) (lower court properly declined to authorize surgery to remove bullet as evidence).

[444]*See, e.g.*, CivPol, art. 19; American, art. 13; European, art. 10. *See generally* ARTICLE 19 WORLD REPORT 1988: INFORMATION, FREEDOM AND CENSORSHIP 291–302 (1988); H. HANNUM, *supra* note 100, at 46–83.

Political Rights and European Convention on Human Rights refer to the special "duties and responsibilities" which attach to exercise of freedom of expression, and freedom of the press may be limited in order, *inter alia*, to protect the rights and reputations of others.[445] At the same time, however, both the Covenant on Civil and Political Rights and European Convention on Human Rights underscore the necessity for a public trial except in specified circumstances.[446]

While the European Commission of Human Rights has found that, "in particular in cases where laymen participate as jurors in the proceedings, this guarantee [of a fair hearing] may be seriously impaired by a virulent press campaign against the accused,"[447] subsequent cases seem to require a very strong showing by an accused of actual prejudice or bias by the trier of fact.[448] The Commission also has noted that trial by a professional judge (as opposed to a jury) "constitutes a further guarantee for impartiality."[449]

As seems to be the case in the United States, decisions of international tribunals as to whether pretrial publicity has been so prejudicial as to violate the requirements of due process or a fair trial are based closely on the particular circumstances of each case, and only rarely are convictions overturned. "[T]he mass media and even the authorities responsible for crime policy, cannot be expected to refrain from all statements, such as the mere existence of criminal proceedings or the fact that a suspicion exists."[450]

---

[445]The leading European cases dealing with limitations on the press are Sunday Times v. U.K., *supra* note 93 (prior restraint on publishing article concerning pending civil suits *re* Thalidomide), and Handyside v. U.K., Eur. Court H.R., Judgment of 7 Dec. 1976, Ser. A No. 24 (obscenity).

[446]CivPol, art. 14(1), provides, *inter alia*, "The Press and the public may be excluded from all or part of a trial for reasons of morals, public order (*ordre public*) or national security in a democratic society, or when the interest of the private lives of the parties so requires, or to the extent strictly necessary in the opinion of the court in special circumstances where publicity would prejudice the interests of justice." Similar language is found in European, art. 6(1).

Compare recent U.S. cases upholding public access to trials and related proceedings, based on the historical tradition of openness and the role of access in enhancing the integrity of the judicial process, e.g., Press Enterprise Co. v. Superior Court (Press Enterprise II), 106 S.Ct. 2735 (1986); Press Enterprise Co. v. Superior Court (Press Enterprise I), 464 U.S. 501 (1984); Globe Newspaper Co. v. Superior Court, 475 U.S. 596 (1982).

[447]X v. Austria, App. No. 1467/63, Eur. Comm. H.R., dec. on admissibility of 23 July 1963, 11 Coll. Dec. 31, 43. Compare the Supreme Court's holding that a fair trial was impossible due to "the massive, pervasive and prejudicial publicity" surrounding the case. Sheppard v. Maxwell, 384 U.S. 333 (1966).

[448]*See* cases excerpted in 2 STRASBOURG DIGEST at 756–59.

[449]*Id. Cf.* X v U.K., App. No. 3860/68, Eur. Comm. H.R., dec. on admissibility of 16 May 1969, 30 Coll. Dec. 70 (noting that an appeals court which has jurisdiction over the merits of a case can correct any errors committed by the trial court jury due to prejudicial publicity). Compare, however, the following observation by the U.S. Supreme Court in Estes v. Texas, 381 U.S. 532 (1965): Even judges "are subject to the same psychological reactions as laymen," and "it is difficult to remain oblivious to the pressures that the news media can bring to bear on them both directly and through the shaping of public opinion."

[450]X v. Netherlands, App. No. 9433/81, Eur. Comm. H.R., dec. on admissibility of 11 Dec. 1981, 27 Dec. & Rep. 233.

Trial Within a Reasonable Time

Even if detention is initially justified, an accused detained on remand must be tried "within a reasonable time".[451]

> The reasonableness of the time spent by an accused person in detention up to the beginning of the trial must be assessed in relation to the very fact of his detention. Until conviction he must be presumed innocent, and the purpose of the provision under consideration [art. 5(3)] is essentially to require his provisional release once his continuing detention ceases to be reasonable.[452]

The European Court of Human Rights declined to adopt a detailed list of seven criteria proposed by the European Commission of Human Rights to judge the "reasonable time" mandated by article 5(3).[453] Instead, the Court has chosen to judge each case in light of the particular circumstances surrounding it, taking into account such factors as the reasons given by the government at the time that applications for release were refused, the agreed facts in the case, the complexity of the situation, and whether the conduct of either the prosecuting authorities or the accused contributed to the delay.[454]

While no firm rules have developed within European jurisprudence, in no case has a period of less than a year between arrest and trial been considered unreasonable. Detention of more than two years pending the conclusion of the trial of first instance has been found to be excessive and a violation of the Convention,[455] while, under other circumstances, longer periods of detention have been upheld.[456]

Most of the jurisprudence of the Human Rights Committee in cases arising under the Covenant on Civil and Political Rights concern Uruguay (during the period of military control in the late 1970s and early 1980s),

---

[451]CivPol, art. 9(3); American, art. 7(5); European, art. 5(3).

[452]Neumeister v. Austria, *supra* note 153, at 37.

[453]The seven criteria were: 1) the actual length of detention; 2) the length of detention on remand in relation to the nature of the offence, the penalty prescribed and to be expected in the case of conviction, and any legal provision for deducting time already served from the sentence imposed; 3) material, moral, or other effects on the accused detainee; 4) the conduct of the accused; 5) any difficulties in investigating the case due to its complexity; 6) the manner in which the investigation was conducted, including whether the authorities demonstrated due diligence; and 7) the conduct of the judicial authorities concerned. *See* Neumeister v. Austria, App. No. 1936/63, Eur. Comm. H.R., Report of 27 May 1966.

[454]Good summaries of the Court's early cases concerning trial within a reasonable time may be found in Cohn, *supra* note 202, at 347–68, 408–25, and Stoiber, *supra* note 180, at 350–55; *also see generally* J. FAWCETT, *supra* note 169, at 105–16, 167–70.

[455]*E.g.*, Neumeister v. Austria, *supra* note 153 [detention of 26 months]; Stögmüller v. Austria, *supra* note 150 [2 years]; Ringeisen v. Austria, *supra* note 150 [2 years].

[456]*E.g.*, Wemhoff v. Austria, *supra* note 151 [41 months]; Schertenleib v. Switzerland, Eur. Comm. H.R., Report of 11 Dec. 1980, 23 Dec. & Rep. 137 [31 months]; Bonnechaux v. Switzerland, App. No. 8224/78, Eur. Comm. H.R., Report of 5 Dec. 1979, 18 Dec. & Rep. 100 [34 months]; Ventura v. Italy, *supra* note 150 [5 years].

and the Committee regularly found violations of the Covenant in the context of lengthy detention without trial under Uruguay's "prompt security measures." As the Uruguayan government rarely responded fully on the merits of individual cases, no issues of alleged complexity of the proceedings, which might have justified the long periods of detention, arose.[457]

The right to be tried "within a reasonable time" is a separate right, and governments may not unreasonably delay the trial even if the accused has been released from detention.[458] This standard parallels the requirement of the Sixth Amendment to the U.S. Constitution, which provides that "[i]n all criminal prosecutions, the accused shall enjoy the right to a speedy and public trial" and is applicable to both federal and state prosecutions through the due process clause of the Fourteenth Amendment.[459]

Under the jurisprudence of the European Convention,[460] this period begins when a person is "charged" with a criminal offense. " 'Charge' . . . may be defined as 'the official notification given to an individual by the competent authority of an allegation that he has committed a criminal offence,' a definition that also corresponds to the test whether 'the situation of the [suspect] has been substantially affected.' " [461] In practice, this may be the date of the accused's arrest,[462] when a preliminary investigation is opened,[463] or when an indictment is filed.[464]

The European Court of Human Rights has indicated that the "reasonable time" within which criminal proceedings must be completed is a somewhat more flexible concept than the similar requirement under article 5(3) of the Convention, which is applicable to an imprisoned suspect.[465] The determination of "reasonableness" depends on the

---

[457] *Cf., e.g.*, Campora v. Uruguay, *supra* note 248 [9 years]; Dermit v. Uruguay, Comm. No. 84/1981, *Report of the Human Rights Committee*, *supra* note 248, at 124 [20 months]; Vasilskis v. Uruguay, *supra* note 248 [5½ years]; Solorzano v. Venezuela, Comm. No. 156/1983, *Report of the Human Rights Committee* (1986), *supra* note 278, at 134 [7 years, 10 months].

[458] CivPol, art. 14(3)(c) ["without undue delay"]; American, art. 8(1); European, art. 6(1); African, art. 7(1)(d).

[459] *See* Klopfer v. North Carolina, 386 U.S. 213 (1967).

[460] *See generally* Eissen, *supra* note 327, at 34–38; cases excerpted in 2 STRASBOURG DIGEST at 502–658.

[461] Eckle v. F.R.G., App. No. 8130/78, Eur. Court H.R., Judgment of 15 July 1982, Ser. A No. 51, at para. 73, citing De Weer v. Belgium, *supra* note 319.

[462] *See, e.g.*, Wemhoff v. F.R.G., *supra* note 151.

[463] *See, e.g.*, Ringeisen v. Austria, *supra* note 150.

[464] *See, e.g.*, Soltikow v. F.R.G., App. No. 2256/64, Eur. Comm. H.R., Report of 3 Feb. 1970, 14 Y.B. EUR. CONV. ON HUMAN RIGHTS 868. The general rule in the U.S. is that the right to a speedy trial attaches at the time of arrest or formal charge, whichever comes first, but not at the pre-indictment stage. *See, e.g.*, U.S. v. Marion, 404 U.S. 307 (1971).

[465] *See* König v. F.R.G., *supra* note 358, at para. 96; Köplinger v. Austria, App. No. 1850/63, Eur. Comm. H.R., Report of 1 Oct. 1968, 12 Y.B. EUR. CONV. ON HUMAN RIGHTS 438, at para. 33.

circumstances of each case and includes consideration of the complexity of the case and the conduct of both the accused[466] and the prosecution. Only where delays are attributable to the government may the European organs find, in appropriate cases, that there has been a failure to comply with the "reasonable time" requirement.[467]

This process of determining "reasonableness" is similar to that employed in the U.S. In the leading case of *Barker v. Wingo*,[468] the Supreme Court articulated a balancing test that identified four criteria as among those which courts should consider in determining whether or not a defendant's right to a speedy trial had been violated: the length of the delay, the reason for the delay, whether and when the defendant asserted the right to a speedy trial, and whether the defendant was prejudiced by the delay.[469] The last criterion is not found in discussions of the international "reasonable time" standard (and need not be affirmatively shown even in the U.S.[470]), and the third would only be of concern in determining whether a complainant to an international body had fulfilled the requirement of exhausting available domestic remedies.

It is difficult to discern precise rules or guidelines from European jurisprudence for determining what is a "reasonable" duration for criminal proceedings, as the European Commission and Court consider each case in detail. Most of the cases involve delays of several years rather than months, although the Commission has found a delay of two years between conviction on traffic offenses and the hearing of an appeal to be excessive.[471] On the other hand, one leading case held that a period of more than seven years from the bringing of charges until a final determination of guilt or innocence was compatible with the requirement of reasonableness.[472]

---

[466]The European Convention does not require a defendant "actively to co-operate with the judicial authorities. Neither can any reproach be levelled against . . . [a defendant] for having made full use of the remedies available under the domestic law. Nonetheless, . . . [defendant's conduct] constitutes an objective fact, not capable of being attributed to the . . . State, which is to be taken into account when determining whether or not the proceedings lasted longer than the reasonable time referred to in Article 5(1)." Eckle v. F.R.G., *supra* note 461, at para. 82. *Cf.* Cates v. U.S., 379 A.2d 968 (D.C.Ct.App. 1977) (denying a speedy trial challenge when the defendant had given the authorities an incorrect name and therefore bore some responsibility for the delay in the proceedings).

[467]Buchholz v. F.R.G., App. No. 7759/77, Eur. Court H.R., Judgment of 6 May 1981, Ser. A No. 42, at para. 49.

[468]407 U.S. 514 (1972).

[469]On the facts of the case, the Court denied Barker's challenge because he failed to assert his right to a speedy trial until late in the proceedings. Barker's trial had been delayed for five years after his arrest, while the government pursued six separate re-trials of a co-conspirator.

[470]Moore v. Arizona, 414 U.S. 25 (1973).

[471]Marijnissen v. Netherlands, App. No. 9193/80, Eur. Comm. H.R., Report of 12 Mar. 1984.

[472]Neumeister v. Austria, *supra* note 153. While observing that seven years was "an exceptionally long period which in most cases should be considered as exceeding the reasonable time laid

These periods include all proceedings through a final determination on appeal;[473] in the United States, however, appeals are not a part of the criminal prosecution to which Sixth Amendment rights attach.[474] With respect to commencement of the initial trial in the United States, "any delay of eight months or longer is deemed 'presumptively prejudicial,' any delay of less than five months is not, while there is judicial disagreement as to the six to seven month range."[475]

Many of the multi-year delays upheld under the European Convention involved large-scale economic crimes or fraud, in which the complexity of the case (and the absence of bad faith on the part of the government) has been found to justify the long periods of investigation and appeal.[476] The existence of a heavy judicial workload seems not to excuse long trial delays,[477] and the European Court of Human Rights also has rejected the existence of violent disorders and an "unusual political and social climate" as excusing otherwise unreasonable delays.[478] "The Court points out that

---

down in Article 6(1)" of the Convention, the Court considered the case to be one of "extraordinary complexity," including difficulties in obtaining evidence from witnesses abroad and a case record consisting of 21 volumes of about 500 pages each and numerous other documents. *Id.* at paras. 19–21.

[473] *See, e.g.*, Wemhoff v. F.R.G., *supra* note 151; Neumeister v. Austria, *supra* note 153.

[474] *See* Douglas v. California, 372 U.S. 353 (1963). A recent Supreme Court case held that the time during which the government appealed a district court's dismissal of an indictment was not to be counted towards determination of the "speedy" trial requirement, where the defendants were not incarcerated nor subject to bail. U.S. v. Loud Hawk, 474 U.S. 302 (1986). However, state appellate review of criminal convictions must meet the requirements of due process and equal protection, and "any substantial retardation of the appellate process" may violate due process. Rheuark v. Shaw, 628 F.2d 297 (5th Cir. 1980); *see* W. LAFAVE & J. ISRAEL, *supra* note 3, at 702–03.

[475] W. LAFAVE & J. ISRAEL, *supra* note 3, at 688–89. Under the Speedy Trial Act of 1974, 18 U.S.C. §§ 3161–74, an indictment or information must be filed within 30 days of arrest and the trial must begin within 70 days from the filing and making public of the indictment or information. However, these periods may be in effect extended by excluding delays resulting from, *inter alia*, "other proceedings concerning the defendant," the absence of essential witnesses, or the complexity of the case itself.

[476] *See, e.g.*, Neumeister v. Austria, *supra* note 153; Ringeisen v. Austria, *supra* note 150 (fraud proceedings of over 5 years); Huber v. Austria, App. No. 4517/70, Eur. Comm. H.R., Report of 8 Feb. 1973, 18 Y.B. EUR. CONV. ON HUMAN RIGHTS 326 (economic crimes involving 23 suspects, operations in several countries, and over 32,000 pages of case files which ultimately required over 12 years to resolve; the accused's own conduct also contributed to the delay). But compare Neubeck v. F.R.G., App. No. 9132/80, Eur. Comm. H.R., Report of 12 Dec. 1983 (total period of nearly 14 years could not be justified, despite "particularly complex" issues involving tax and bankruptcy proceedings, requests for assistance from foreign governments, and the accused's "querulous" attitude). *See generally* cases excerpted in 2 STRASBOURG DIGEST at 578–609, 646–58.

[477] *See, e.g.*, Eckle v. F.R.G., *supra* note 461. But compare Buchholz v. F.R.G., *supra* note 467, where no violation was found in view of the government's attempts to expedite cases during a period of heavy demands on the judicial system that were "exceptional in character". Under the U.S. rule enunciated in *Barker*, *supra* note 468, "negligence or overcrowded courts" are considered to be "neutral" reasons for delay, which "nevertheless should be considered since the ultimate responsibility for such circumstances must rest with the government. . . ."

[478] *See* Foti et al. v. Italy, Apps. No. 7604/76 etc., Eur. Court H.R., Judgment of 10 Dec. 1982, Ser. A No. 56 (approximately 20 months after committal for trial without any action by the trial court).

the Convention places a duty on the Contracting States to organise their legal systems so as to allow the courts to comply with the requirements of Article 6(1) including that of trial within a 'reasonable time.' Nonetheless, a temporary backlog of business does not involve liability on the part of the Contracting States provided they have taken reasonably prompt remedial action to deal with an exceptional situation of this kind."[479]

Most of the cases considered by the Human Rights Committee concern detention without trial, and the Committee has not generally distinguished between violations of the right of a detainee to be brought promptly before a judge and the right of a criminal accused to be tried without undue delay.[480] One case in which there was a ten-month delay between arrest and trial was deemed to violate the latter right.[481]

Criminal Versus Other Proceedings

Disciplinary Proceedings

National and international law and practice recognize that persons within certain categories, such as members of the military and prisoners, may be subject to punishment for breaches of discipline which do not rise to the level of criminal conduct. Article 15 of the U.S. Uniform Code of Military Justice[482] permits a commanding officer to impose certain disciplinary punishments – such as restriction to certain areas, arrest in quarters, forfeiture of pay, correctional custody, and extra duties – without the intervention of court-martial. Before a punishment is imposed, the alleged offender can demand trial by court-martial in lieu of the punishment, and persons who consider their punishment unjust or disproportionate to the offense may appeal to the next superior authority. The appeal must be promptly forwarded and decided, but the person punished may in the meantime be required to undergo the punishment adjudged.

Nonjudicial punishment is an administrative method of dealing with minor offenses, not a criminal proceeding, and thus members of the military subjected to such punishment are not protected by the Fifth and Sixth Amendments.[483] Commanding officers have broad discretion in determining whether an alleged offense is sufficiently serious to warrant

---

[479]Buchholz v. F.R.G., *supra* note 467, at para. 51.

[480]*See* deZayas, Möller & Opsahl, *Application by the Human Rights Committee of the International Covenant on Civil and Political Rights Under the Optional Protocol*, 3 CANADIAN HUM. RTS. Y.B. 101, 140.

[481]Drescher Caldas v. Uruguay, Comm. No. 43/1979, *Report of the Human Rights Committee*, *supra* note 248, at 192.

[482]Codified at 10 U.S.C. §§ 801–940.

[483]U.S. v. Penn, 4 M.J. 879 (1978); *see also* Dumas v. U.S., 620 F.2d 247 (3rd Cir. 1980).

court-martial rather than nonjudicial punishment,[484] and review by the Federal Court of Appeals is limited in part to determining whether there was compliance with the requirements of the Uniform Code of Military Justice and certain procedural regulations.[485]

The Supreme Court recently reinstated the common law rule that military courts-martial had jurisdiction over virtually all crimes committed by members of the military,[486] although the 1983 Military Justice Act gives the Supreme Court direct appellate review of courts-martial cases.[487] Under international human rights norms, such military trials for criminal offenses would have to fulfill all the requirements of a fair trial before an independent and impartial tribunal, including the various rights of the defense.

Military disciplinary measures are not excluded from the protection of the European Convention on Human Rights, although the normal restrictions on liberty inherent in military service are specifically permitted by article 4(3)(b) of the Convention (which excludes military service from the general prohibition against forced or compulsory labor). However, article 5 *is* applicable to disciplinary penalties or restrictions "that clearly deviate from the normal conditions of life within the armed forces of the Contracting States. In order to establish whether this is so, account should be taken of a whole range of factors such as the nature, duration, effects and manner of execution of the penalty or measure in question."[488]

Applying these criteria on a case-by-case basis, the Court or Commission has found that "light arrest" (confinement to military camp during off-duty as well as on-duty hours) does not constitute a deprivation of liberty (and thus need not be subject to judicial review), while "aggravated arrest" (confinement to a punishment room with others), "strict arrest" (solitary confinement in a cell), and assignment to a "disciplinary unit" go beyond the normal requirements of military service and therefore are "deprivations of liberty" subject to the procedural and other requirements of article 5 of the Convention.[489]

Several European cases have considered the distinction between disciplinary and criminal offenses, as the full panoply of fair trial guarantees apply only to the latter. The leading case, *Engel et al. v. Nether-*

---

[484]Cappella v. U.S., 624 F.2d 976 (Ct.Cl. 1980).

[485]Hagarty v. U.S., 449 F.2d 352 (Ct.Cl. 1971).

[486]Solorio v. U.S., 107 S.Ct. 2924 (1987) (overruling O'Callahan v. Parker, 395 U.S. 258 (1969)).

[487]Pub. L. No. 98-209, § 10, 97 Stat. 1393, 1405-1406 (codified at 28 U.S.C. § 1259 (1988)).

[488]Engel et al. v. Netherlands, *infra* note 490, at 25.

[489]*Id. Cf.* Eggs v. Switzerland, App. No. 7341/76, Eur. Comm. H.R., Report of 4 Mar. 1978, 15 Dec. & Rep. 35; Santschi et al. v. Switzerland, Apps. Nos. 7468/76 et al., Eur. Comm. H.R., Report of 13 Oct. 1981.

lands,[490] considered various penalties imposed on several Dutch soldiers by their superior officers and set forth the following basic criteria:

> All the Contracting States make a distinction of long standing, albeit in different forms and degrees, between disciplinary proceedings and criminal proceedings. For the individuals affected, the former usually offer substantial advantages in comparison with the latter, for example with regard to the sentences passed. Disciplinary sentences, in general less severe, do not appear in the person's criminal record and entail more limited consequences. It may nevertheless be otherwise; moreover, criminal proceedings are ordinarily accompanied by fuller guarantees.
>
> It must thus be asked whether or not the solution adopted in this connection at the national level is decisive from the standpoint of the Convention. Does Article 6 cease to be applicable just because the competent organs of a Contracting State classify as disciplinary an act or omission and the proceedings it takes against the author, or does it, on the contrary, apply in certain cases notwithstanding this classification?. . . .
>
> The Convention without any doubt allows the States, in the performance of their function as guardians of the public interest, to maintain or establish a distinction between criminal law and disciplinary law, and to draw the dividing line, but only subject to certain conditions. The Convention leaves the States free to designate as a criminal offence an act or commission not constituting the normal exercise of one of the rights that it protects. This is made especially clear by Article 7 [prohibiting *ex post facto* laws]. Such a choice, which has the effect of rendering applicable Articles 6 and 7, in principle escapes supervision by the Court.
>
> The converse choice, for its part, is subject to stricter rules. If the Contracting States were able at their discretion to classify an offence as disciplinary instead of criminal, or to prosecute the author of a "mixed" offence on the disciplinary rather than on the criminal plane, the operation of the fundamental clauses of Articles 6 and 7 would be subordinated to their sovereign will. A latitude extending thus far might lead to results incompatible with the purpose and object of the Convention. The Court therefore has jurisdiction . . . to satisfy itself that the disciplinary does not improperly encroach upon the criminal. . . .
>
> [In order to determine whether an offence is disciplinary or

[490] Apps. Nos. 5100/71 et al., Eur. Court H.R., Judgment of 8 June 1976, Ser. A No. 22.

criminal,] it is first necessary to know whether the provision(s) defining the offence charged belong, according to the legal system of the respondent State, to criminal law, disciplinary law or both concurrently. This however provides no more than a starting point. The indications so afforded have only a formal and relative value and must be examined in the light of the common denominator of the respective legislation of the various Contracting States.

> The very nature of the offence is a factor of greater import. When a serviceman finds himself accused of an act or omission allegedly contravening a legal rule governing the operation of the armed forces, the State may in principle employ against him disciplinary law rather than criminal law. . . .
>
> However, supervision by the Court does not stop there. Such supervision would generally prove to be illusory if it did not also take into consideration the degree of severity of the penalty that the person concerned risks incurring. In a society subscribing to the rule of law, there belong to the "criminal" sphere deprivations of liberty liable to be imposed as a punishment, except those which by their nature, duration or manner of execution cannot be appreciably detrimental. The seriousness of what is at stake, the traditions of the Contracting States and the importance attached by the Convention to respect for the physical liberty of the person all require that this should be so.[491]

These three criteria—the domestic designation as disciplinary or criminal, the inherent nature of the offence, and the severity of the penalty—have subsequently been utilized in cases involving prison discipline[492] and the decriminalization of petty offenses, such as traffic fines.[493] This might be compared with the U.S. focus on whether a statute is "essentially penal in nature," which is utilized in order to determine whether criminal procedure must be followed by a state which wishes to take a particular action.[494] The factors found to be significant for purposes of the U.S. analysis include: 1) whether the potential sanction involves an affirmative disability or restraint; 2) whether the penalty has been regarded historically as a punishment; 3) whether the imposition of the

---

[491]*Id.* at paras. 80–83.

[492]*See* Campbell & Fell v. U.K., App. No. 7511/76, Eur. Court H.R., Judgment of 28 June 1984, Ser. A No. 80.

[493]*See* Oztürk v. F.R.G., *infra* note 497.

[494]Kennedy v. Mendoza-Martinez, 372 U.S. 144, 164 (1963) (automatic deprivation of citizenship for leaving the country to avoid military service during wartime).

sanction depends on a finding of scienter; 4) whether the traditional purposes of punishment are served; 5) whether the behavior at issue is already criminal; 6) whether there may be an alternative purpose for the sanction; and 7) whether the sanction seems excessive in relation to any alternative purpose.[495] Unlike the situation in Europe, conclusive evidence of legislative intent regarding the penal nature of a statute also is extremely relevant.[496]

Decriminalized or Regulatory Offenses

The European Court of Human Rights generally has required that due process rights be guaranteed, at least at an appellate level, even for minor "decriminalized" offenses. For example, several cases considered amendments to the German penal code which reclassified many minor traffic and other "offenses" as separate, non-criminal "regulatory offenses" in which the maximum penalty is payment of a fine.

> By removing certain forms of conduct from the category of criminal offenses under domestic law, the law-maker may be able to serve the interests of the individual as well as the needs of the proper administration of justice, in particular in so far as the judicial authorities are thereby relieved of the task of prosecuting and punishing contraventions – which are numerous but of minor importance – of road traffic rules. The Convention is not opposed to the moves towards "decriminalisation" which are taking place – in extremely varied forms – in the member States of the Council of Europe. . . .
>
> Nonetheless, the Court would firstly note that, according to the ordinary meaning of the terms, there generally come within the ambit of the criminal law offenses that make their perpetrator liable to penalties intended, *inter alia*, to be deterrent and usually consisting of fines and of measures depriving the person of his liberty.
>
> In addition, misconduct of the kind committed by [the applicant] continues to be classified as part of the criminal law in the vast majority of the Contracting States . . . ; such misconduct [careless driving and causing damage to another vehicle], being regarded as illegal and reprehensible, is punishable by criminal penalties.
>
> Moreover, the changes resulting from the 1968/1975 [German] legislation relate essentially to procedural matters and to the range of sanctions. . . . [The fine which may be imposed] retained a punitive character, which is the customary distin-

---

[495] *Id.* at 168–69.

[496] *Id.* at 169; *compare* Engel et al. v. Netherlands, *supra* note 490.

guishing feature of criminal penalties. The rule of law infringed by the applicant has, for its part, undergone no change of content. It is a rule that is directed, not towards a given group possessing a special status—in the manner, for example, of disciplinary law —but towards all citizens in their capacity as road-users; it prescribes conduct of a certain kind and makes the resultant requirement subject to a sanction that is punitive. Indeed, the sanction—and this the Government did not contest—seeks to punish as well as to deter. . . . Above all, the general character of the rule and the purpose of the penalty, being both deterrent and punitive, suffice to show that the offence in question was, in terms of Article 6 of the Convention, criminal in nature.

The fact that it was admittedly a minor offence hardly likely to harm the reputation of the offender does not take it outside the ambit of Article 6. There is in fact nothing to suggest that the criminal offence referred to in the Convention necessarily implies a certain degree of seriousness. . . .

It in no wise follows from this [holding that article 6 is applicable] . . . that the very principle of the system adopted in the matter by the German legislature is being put in question. Having regard to the large number of minor offenses, notably in the sphere of road traffic, a Contracting State may have good cause for relieving its courts of the task of their prosecution and punishment. Conferring the prosecution and punishment of minor offenses on administrative authorities is not inconsistent with the Convention provided that the person concerned is enabled to take any decision thus made against him before a tribunal that does offer the guarantees of Article 6.[497]

The European Commission of Human Rights subsequently reaffirmed that a tribunal affording the safeguards provided for in article 6 of the European Convention must be available to an accused to consider questions of both law and fact, although it is sufficient if such a tribunal is available to review an initial administrative determination rather than at the trial court level.[498]

---

[497]Oztürk v. F.R.G., App. No. 8544/79, Eur. Court H.R., Judgment of 21 Feb. 1984, Ser. A No. 73, at paras. 49-56.

[498]*See* Belilos v. Switzerland, App. No. 10328/83, Eur. Comm. H.R., Report of 7 May 1986.

Double Jeopardy

The Fifth Amendment to the U.S. Constitution declares that no one shall "be subject for the same offence to be twice put in jeopardy of life or limb," and this prohibition has been held to be fully applicable to the states.[499] Corresponding provisions appear in several international instruments.[500]

In his submittal of the Covenant on Civil and Political Rights to the Senate for advice and consent, President Carter included an understanding that the Covenant's provision on double jeopardy "is applicable only when the judgment of acquittal has been rendered by a court of the same governmental unit."[501] This corresponds to the U.S. constitutional standard that permits retrial if a person has been acquitted of the same crime in another "sovereign" jurisdiction (i.e., by a state or the federal government),[502] although state law may prohibit such action. International bodies have applied a similar rule to prosecutions by different countries for the same offence, holding that the international prohibition against double jeopardy applies only to prosecutions within a given country.[503]

Of course, international law applies to the states as well as to the federal government,[504] and the Covenant on Civil and Political Rights provides specifically that it "shall extend to all parts of federal States without any limitations or exceptions."[505] While the U.S. "dual sovereignty" theory would therefore not be acceptable under international law,[506] the United States also has suggested a general reservation to this provision of the Covenant.[507]

---

[499]*See* Benton v. Maryland, 395 U.S. 784 (1969).

[500]CivPol, art. 14(7) (no retrial after final conviction or acquittal); American, art. 8(4) (no retrial after final acquittal). Neither the European nor African human rights treaties contain corresponding provisions.

[501]Message of the President, *supra* note 20, at xiii. A corresponding understanding is set forth with respect to art. 8(4) of the American Convention. *Id.* at xix.

[502]*See* Heath v. Alabama, 474 U.S. 82 (1985) (state prosecution after federal acquittal); Abbate v. U.S., 359 U.S. 187 (1959) (federal prosecution after state prosecution); Bartkus v. Illinois, 359 U.S. 121 (1959) (prosecutions by different states).

[503]*See* A.P. v. Italy, Comm. No. 204/1986, *Report of the Human Rights Committee, supra* note 427, at 242.

[504]*See* discussion *supra*, at 10–12.

[505]CivPol, art. 50. Compare American, art. 28, which provides that national governments are to implement all of the convention's provisions "over whose subject matter it [the national government] exercises legislative and judicial jurisdiction." With respect to matters falling within state jurisdiction, the federal government is to take "suitable measures, in accordance with its constitution and its laws, to the end that the competent authorities of the constituent units may adopt appropriate provisions" to fulfill the convention.

[506]*Also see* Vienna Convention on the Law of Treaties, *supra* note 59, art. 27; RESTATEMENT § 115 comment b at 64.

[507]Message of the President, *supra* note 20, at xiv.

PRISONERS' RIGHTS

The U.S. Supreme Court has rarely found constitutionally based liberty interests to be present in the prison context.[508] If such an interest is found, the state may only restrict it or take it away through procedures which will prevent arbitrariness. In *Vitek v. Jones*,[509] for example, the Supreme Court held that prisoners have a constitutionally based liberty interest in not being classified as mentally ill. The state, therefore, has to provide due process protections before committing a prisoner to a mental hospital. Similarly, in *Procunier v. Martinez*,[510] the Court held that prisoners have a First Amendment based liberty interest in uncensored mail. Thus, prisoners are entitled to due process protections when prison officials censor their mail.

There are no "implied" limitations on the rights of prisoners under the European human rights system,[511] although the European Convention contains numerous clauses which permit the restriction of rights on grounds of, *inter alia*, public safety, preventing crime or disorder, or protecting the rights of others. Thus, restrictions on prisoners' rights (assuming that the right asserted is guaranteed under the European Convention) can only be justified by reference to a specific provision in the Convention. A similar situation prevails with respect to other international instruments: it is assumed that prisoners have the same rights as all other persons, subject to those restrictions which can be justified by the government or which are otherwise inherent in the concept of detention or imprisonment.

Access to the Courts

While a U.S. defendant may have a constitutional right to counsel only at the first level of appellate review,[512] the Supreme Court also has held that "prisoners have a constitutional right of access to the courts"

---

[508] *See* Hewitt v. Helms, 459 U.S. 460 (1983).

[509] 445 U.S. 480 (1980).

[510] Note 531 *infra*.

[511] *See* Golder v. U.K., App. No. 4451/70, Eur. Court H.R., Judgment of 21 Feb. 1975, Ser. A No. 18, at paras. 44–45.

[512] *See* discussion *supra* at 85–89.

which must be "adequate, effective, and meaningful".[513] "[R]egulations and practices that unjustifiably obstruct the availability of professional representation or other aspects of the right of access to the courts are invalid."[514]

International jurisprudence follows a similar line of analysis, although a case may focus on specifically guaranteed rights (such as the right to respect for correspondence) in addition to or instead of more general provisions on access to a fair and independent tribunal in the determination of "civil rights and obligations" or any "criminal charge". The Covenant on Civil and Political Rights and American Convention on Human Rights provide a right to appeal from a conviction;[515] the European Convention does not.[516]

Correspondence

The right to correspond is a First Amendment liberty interest protected by due process.[517] Prisoners must be notified when letters to or from them are rejected, the author of the letter must be given a "reasonable opportunity to protest," and complaints must be administered by someone other than the censor.[518]

International human rights law specifically protects the right to respect for correspondence.[519] In interpreting the Covenant on Civil and Political Rights, the Human Rights Committee has accepted "that it is normal for prison authorities to exercise measures of control and censorship over prisoners' correspondence," but it goes on to note that any such measures should be "subject to satisfactory legal safeguards against arbitrary application."[520] Citing the Covenant provision which requires humane treatment of prisoners (article 10), the Committee observed that, in particular, "prisoners should be allowed under necessary supervision to communicate with their family and reputable friends at regular intervals, by correspondence as well as by receiving visits."[521]

---

[513]Bounds v. Smith, 430 U.S. 817, 822 (1977).

[514]Procunier v. Martinez, *infra* note 531, at 419.

[515]CivPol, art. 14(5); American, art. 8(2)(h).

[516]However, any appellate system established must respect the "fundamental guarantees" of art. 6 of the European Convention, *i.e.*, a fair trial. *See* Delcourt v. Belgium, *supra* note 330; *cf.* Oztürk v. F.R.G., *supra* note 497. These guarantees do not apply to proceedings before constitutional courts, which in civil law systems generally have separate jurisdiction from courts of cassation or other courts which consider non-constitutional challenges. *See* X v. F.R.G., App. No. 8961/80, Eur. Comm. H.R., dec. on admissibility of 8 Dec. 1981, 26 Dec. & Rep. 200.

[517]Procunier v. Martinez, *infra* note 531.

[518]*Id.* at 417–19.

[519]CivPol, art. 17(1); American, art. 11(2); European, art. 8(1).

[520]Angel Estrella v. Uruguay, *supra* note 248, at para. 9.2.

[521]*Id.*

In an earlier case, the Human Rights Committee had found that a Canadian statute which permitted censorship by a prison warden of any letter (except certain letters to or from a lawyer) "on the ground that its contents are objectionable or that the letter is of excessive length" did not "in itself provide satisfactory legal safeguards against arbitrary application."[522] Subsequently adopted regulations, which the Committee deemed to be compatible with the Covenant, exempted privileged correspondence (e.g., letters to legislators and lawyers) from any censorship or control, and subjected other correspondence to censorship if it threatened "the management, operation, discipline or security" of the prison.[523]

The rights of privacy and correspondence may be limited under the European Convention on Human Rights "in accordance with the law and . . . [when] necessary in a democratic society in the interests of national security, public safety or the economic well-being of the country, for the prevention of disorder or crime, for the protection of health or morals, or for the protection of the rights and freedoms of others."[524] Like the Human Rights Committee, the European Commission and Court of Human Rights have observed that some restrictions on correspondence are inherent with respect to detained persons, and, in *Silver and others v. U.K.*,[525] the European Commission addressed a series of restrictions imposed by British prison authorities on prisoners' letters.

The Commission held that stopping letters based on the following practices did not fall within the range of restrictions permitted under the Convention: a rule requiring "prior internal ventilation" of complaints about prison treatment before external complaints were permitted; the prohibition of letters to legal representatives or in connection with business matters without permission of the Secretary of State; and general or blanket prohibitions against letters containing complaints or representations about a prisoner's trial, conviction, or sentence, or addressed to other than relatives and friends, or against material intended for publication, which attempts to stimulate public petition, which contains grossly improper language, or which is deliberately calculated to hold the prison authorities up to contempt. However, the Commission upheld the right of prison authorities to prohibit letters which attempt to stimulate "public agitation," circumvent prison regulations, threaten violence, or discuss crime in general or the crime of others.[526] In each instance, the Commis-

---

[522]Pinkney v. Canada, Comm. No. 27/1978, *Report of the Human Rights Committee, supra* note 138, at 101, *reprinted in Selected Decisions, supra* note 139, at 95, at paras. 31, 34.

[523]*Id.* at paras. 31-32.

[524]European, art. 8(2).

[525]Apps. Nos. 5947/72 etc., Eur. Comm. H.R., Report of 11 Oct. 1980; the European Court reached similar findings, Judgment of 25 Mar. 1983, Ser. A No. 61.

[526]*Id.* at paras. 262-422.

sion balanced the justifications put forward by the authorities with the specific language of the Convention, in the context of construing narrowly the permissibie restrictions.[527]

It might be noted that these cases concerned prohibition of letters rather than only censorship, and "the 'necessity' for interference with the exercise of the right of a convicted prisoner to respect for his correspondence must be appreciated having regard to the ordinary and reasonable requirements of imprisonment."[528] The requirement that restrictions be "necessary in a democratic society" also implies that any limitations be proportionate to the legitimate aim pursued,[529] but "mere supervision" of prisoners' correspondence is generally justified.[530]

Freedom of Information

In *Procunier v. Martinez*,[531] the U.S. Supreme Court set forth a two-pronged test for evaluating prison restrictions on First Amendment rights: 1) the restriction must further a substantial government interest unrelated to the suppression of expression; and 2) the limitation of First Amendment freedoms must be no greater than is necessary to protect that government interest. This standard is quite similar, although expressed in different terms, to international norms, such as the European Convention on Human Rights; the latter requires that a restriction be "necessary in a democratic society," identifies the governmental interests which may be legitimately protected (e.g., public safety), and also requires that the measures taken be proportionate.

Censorship of reading material sent to prisoners has been held to implicate due process rights; prisoners must receive notice of any censorship and an opportunity to be heard, a statement of the reasons for the censorship, a quick decision, and the right to appeal to a prison official other than the censor.[532] Unlike U.S. courts, international bodies seem less concerned with whether restrictions are content-neutral, although censorship based on purely political grounds would probably be incompatible with the European Convention and similar instruments.

The European Commission of Human Rights has generally upheld restrictions placed on materials received by prisoners. It has described a

---

[527] *See, e.g.*, Schönenberger & Durmaz v. Switzerland, App. No. 11368/85, Eur. Court H.R., Judgment of 20 June 1988, Ser. A No. 137.

[528] Golder v. U.K., *supra* note 511, at para. 45.

[529] *See* Handyside v. U.K., *supra* note 445, at paras. 48–50.

[530] Silver and others v. U.K., *supra* note 525, at para. 424.

[531] 416 U.S. 396 (1974).

[532] *See, e.g.*, Hopkins v. Collins, 548 F.2d 503, 504 (4th Cir. 1977); Jackson v. Ward, 458 F. Supp. 546, 565 (W.D.N.Y. 1978).

basic reading allowance of one newspaper per day and seven periodicals or magazines per week as "quite adequate," and it also has upheld rules which restrict publications to those from "recognised source[s]".[533]

> [T]he essence of the applicant's case is that he wishes to receive periodicals, which are generally in a language other than English, from sources that the prison authorities cannot easily check. He has never really explained why he cannot receive these periodicals from an authorised source. . . .
>
> What the applicant is really saying is that he does not want to use up his ordinary entitlement [to periodicals] with regular copies of these magazines. He wants occasional copies sent to him from unrecognised sources. This naturally places considerable strain on the prison authorities who would need to examine foreign language publications for possible messages etc. . . . .
>
> Article 10(2) allows restrictions on the right to receive information if such restrictions are prescribed by law . . . and are necessary in a democratic society for the prevention of disorder or crime. The Commission considers that the restrictions in the present case fall well within this definition. They appear to be designed to prevent the passing of messages (and other material) to prisoners and to make it possible to check incoming material without putting any unnecessary burden on prison staff.[534]

On the facts of the cases presented to it, the Commission has likewise failed to find a violation of a prisoner's rights under the Convention in respect of complaints regarding a lack of writing paper and a typewriter,[535] restricted access to relevant legal texts,[536] or the prohibition of visits from certain newspaper reporters.[537]

---

[533]*See* X v. U.K., App. No. 5270/71, Eur. Comm. H.R., dec. on admissibility of 8 July 1974, 46 Coll. Dec. 54. *Also see* X v. F.R.G., App. No. 4676/70, Eur. Comm. H.R., dec. on admissibility of 31 Mar. 1971 (unpublished), *excerpts reprinted in* 3 STRASBOURG DIGEST at 436–37. Compare Bell v. Wolfish, 441 U.S. 520 (1979), in which the Supreme Court upheld a similar rule barring the receipt of hardcover books by prisoners from anyone except the publisher, a book club, or a bookstore.

[534]X v. U.K., *supra* note 533, at 59–60.

[535]X v. Austria, App. No. 666/59, Eur. Comm. H.R., dec. on admissibility of 17 Mar. 1961 (unpublished), *excerpts reprinted in* 3 STRASBOURG DIGEST at 433.

[536]*See* X v. F.R.G., App. No. 2795/66, Eur. Comm. H.R., dec. on admissibility of 22 May 1969, 12 Y.B. EUR. CONV. ON HUMAN RIGHTS at 192. The U.S. Supreme Court has held that prison authorities must "assist inmates in the preparation and filing of meaningful legal papers by providing prisoners with adequate law libraries or adequate assistance from persons trained in the law." Bounds v. Smith, *supra* note 513, at 828.

[537]X v. Belgium, App. No. 3914/69, Eur. Comm. H.R., dec. on admissibility of 6 Feb. 1970, 34 Coll. Dec. 20. Compare Pell v. Procunier, 417 U.S. 817 (1974), where the Supreme Court upheld a rule that prohibited media interviews with individual prisoners. Although holding that a prisoner retains those First Amendment rights which are not inconsistent with his status as a prisoner or with the objectives of the penal system, the Court upheld the rule on the grounds that there were other ways to communicate with the press, that there were legitimate security concerns, and that the prohibition was not based on the content of the expression.

Rights to Family and Marriage

The European Commission of Human Rights has rejected as ill-founded numerous cases which allege that imprisonment of a convicted prisoner interferes with respect for family life, noting that "the separation of a prisoner from his family and the hardship resulting from it are inherent consequences of the execution of a sentence".[538] However, the Commission has as consistently held that, under ordinary circumstances, a prisoner's right to marry must be respected despite the fact that he or she is in prison.[539]

In the leading case of *Hamer v. U.K.*,[540] the position of a prisoner was distinguished from that of a priest or other person who, of his own free will, places himself in a position where he cannot marry.

> [A] person deprived of his liberty . . . remains in principle entitled to the right to marry and . . . any restriction or regulation of the exercise of that right must not be such as to injure its substance. . . .
>
> Personal liberty is not a necessary pre-condition to the exercise of the right to marry. The practice of States in allowing prisoners to marry, either within prison or on temporary release under escort, shows that no specially onerous or complex arrangements are necessary. The exercise of the right, particularly within a prison, does not, as the Commission has already pointed out, involve the prisoner escaping from the supervision and control of the prison authorities.
>
> Some administrative arrangements must of course be made by the prison authorities before a prisoner can marry. However this also applies to other Convention rights, such as the right of access to court and the right to respect for correspondence and family life. Some positive action is required on the part of the prison authorities to make these rights effective. . . .

---

[538] X v. Austria, App. No. 2676/65, Eur. Comm. H.R., dec. on admissibility of 3 Apr. 1967, 23 Coll. Dec. 31, 37; also see excerpts collected in 3 STRASBOURG DIGEST 119–27.

[539] Article 12 of the European Convention on Human Rights provides: "Men and women of marriageable age have the right to marry and to found a family, according to the national laws governing the exercise of this right." Similar provisions may be found in CivPol, art. 23, and American, art. 17.

[540] App. No. 7114/75, Eur. Comm. H.R., Report of 13 Dec. 1979, 24 Dec. & Rep. 5. *Also see* Draper v. U.K., App. No. 8186/78, Eur. Comm. H.R., Report of 10 July 1980, 24 Dec. & Rep. 72 (prohibition on marriage by prisoners serving a life sentence violates right to marry). These cases would appear to overrule an earlier decision, in which the Commission upheld the refusal of German prison authorities to permit a prisoner's marriage and suggested that such a decision could take into account, *inter alia*, the length of the prisoner's sentence and the fact that "marriage of prisoners inevitably affected the maintenance of order within prison establishments". *See* X v. F.R.G., App. No. 892/60, Eur. Comm. H.R., dec. on admissibility of 13 Apr. 1961, 4 Y.B. EUR. CONV. ON HUMAN RIGHTS 240.

> The essence of the right to marry . . . is the formation of a legally binding association between a man and a woman. It is for them to decide whether or not they wish to enter such an association in circumstances where they cannot cohabit.[541]

The right to found a family has not been extended to conjugal visits in prisons, even though this right (like the right to marry) is not subject to restriction on the grounds of, e.g., public order. Through an analysis seemingly inconsistent with the marriage cases referred to above, the European Commission of Human Rights has held that the right to found a family "does not mean that a person must at all times be given the actual possibility to procreate his descendants. It would seem that the situation of a lawfully convicted person detained in prison . . . falls under his own responsibility, and that his right to found a family has not otherwise been infringed."[542]

A subsequent case was a bit more nuanced, as the Commission noted "with sympathy" reforms that increased the possibilities for conjugal visits (although the Commission also noted that it was not the general practice among state parties to the Convention to permit sexual relations in prison).[543] "The Commission accepts that in fact the security and good order in prison would be seriously endangered if all married prisoners were allowed to keep up their conjugal life in the prison."[544] However, the Commission has held that preventing a person temporarily detained *in-communicado* from contacting his wife for a period of 45 hours violates the Convention's guarantee of respect for family life.[545]

---

[541]Hamer v. U.K., *supra* note 540, at paras. 63-73.

[542]X v. U.K., App. No. 6564/74, Eur. Comm. H.R., dec. on admissibility of 21 May 1975, 2 Dec. & Rep. 105, 106.

[543]X & Y v. Switzerland, App. No. 8166/78, Eur. Comm. H.R., dec. on admissibility of 3 oct. 1978, 13 Dec. & Rep. 241. *Also see* X v. F.R.G., App. No. 3603/68, Eur. Comm. H.R., dec. on admissibility of 4 Feb. 1970, 31 Coll. Dec. 48.

[544]X & Y v. Switzerland, *supra* note 543, at 242.

[545]*See* McVeigh, Evans & O'Neill v. U.K., Eur. Comm. H.R., *supra* note 182, at paras. 62-70, 233-39.

Administrative Segregation and Transfer

In *Hewitt v. Helms*, the Supreme Court found that "administrative segregation was the sort of confinement that inmates should reasonably anticipate receiving," and accordingly held that there was no constitutionally based liberty interest in remaining in the general prison population (unless specific statutes or regulations had created a protected interest).[546] A similar situation prevails with respect to transfers or classifications for various prison programs.[547]

The European Commission of Human Rights has observed that the transfer of a prisoner further away from home[548] or, "under certain circumstances," even the refusal to transfer a prisoner closer to the prisoner's family[549] might violate the European Convention's guarantee of respect for family life. However, no such violation has been found on the facts of any case presented to the Commission.[550]

The Commission has termed the classification of prisoners "a reasonable measure of prison administration."[551] While the Commission has considered in detail several applications challenging classifications (most of which allege violations of the prohibition against inhuman or degrading treatment or punishment[552]), it would appear that only grossly arbitrary decisions might be considered incompatible with administrative discretion.[553]

---

[546]*Supra* note 508, at 466–68.

[547]*See, e.g.*, Meachum v. Fano, 427 U.S. 215 (1976) (transfers) Montayne v. Haymes, 427 U.S. 236 (1976) (same); Neal v. Director, District of Columbia Dept. of Corrections, 684 F.2d 17 (D.C. Cir. 1982) (same); Vitek v. Jones, *supra* note 509 (same, recognizing some due process rights before a transfer); Hardwick v. Ault, 447 F. Supp 116 (M.D. Ga. 1978) (same); Moody v. Daggett, 429 U.S. 78 (1976) (classification of prisoners).

[548]*See, e.g.*, X v. U.K., app. 7645/76, Eur. Comm. H.R., dec. on admissibility of 2 May 1978 (unpublished), *excerpts reprinted in* 3 STRASBOURG DIGEST 124–25.

[549]X v. U.K., App. No. 8586/79, Eur. Comm. H.R., dec. on admissibility of 10 Oct. 1980 (unpublished), *excerpts reprinted in* 3 STRASBOURG DIGEST 126.

[550]*Cf.* X v. U.K., App. No. 5712/72, Eur. Comm. H.R., dec. on admissibility of 18 July 1974, 46 Coll. Dec. 112 (detention in U.K. of prisoner from and convicted in the Bahamas upheld because no appropriate facility existed in the Bahamas). "The question becomes one of balance and reasonableness. There is no suggestion that the applicant's family life has been interfered with merely because of administrative convenience. He has been moved to, and is kept in, a place far from his home because there is no place near to his home where he can be kept in reasonable security." *Id.* at 116.

[551]X v. U.K., App. No. 7610/76, Eur. Comm. H.R., dec. on admissibility of 9 Oct. 1979 (unpublished), *excerpts reprinted in* 1 STRASBOURG DIGEST 157.

[552]*Cf.* discussion *supra* at 59–63.

[553]*See, e.g.*, X v. U.K., App. No. 6363/73, Eur. Comm. H.R., dec. on admissibility of 4 Mar. 1976 (unpublished), *excerpts reprinted in* 1 STRASBOURG DIGEST 156–57 (possible violation if classification "wholly unjustified"); X v. U.K., App. No. 5265/71, Eur. Comm. H.R., dec. on admissibility of 29 Sept. 1975, 3 Dec. & Rep. 5 (although government's observations on the question of classification were "vague," decision on classification was "not unfounded").

Parole

In the United States, due process protections are required only if prison regulations or state statutes have created a protectable liberty interest. For example, such an interest has been found where a statute provided that a parole board "shall" release a prisoner, subject to certain restrictions.[554]

The Supreme Court has held that there is a constitutionally based liberty interest entitling parolees to procedural due process before parole can be *revoked*.[555] In *granting* parole, conversely, there is no liberty interest unless one is created by statute or regulation.[556] In *Morrissey v. Brewer*, the Court stated that parole revocation requires an informal hearing process which must include written notice of the claimed violations of parole, disclosure of the evidence against the parolee, a neutral and detached hearing body, the opportunity to be heard in person and to present witnesses, the right to confront adverse witnesses (unless the hearing body specifically finds good cause for not allowing confrontation), and a written statement by the hearing body citing the reasons for its decision.[557]

In *Greenholtz*, the Supreme Court determined that whether a state provides a protectable entitlement in its procedures for granting parole must be decided on a case-by-case basis.[558] The mere possibility of parole is not sufficient to entitle a prisoner to due process protections; the language of the statute must create an expectation of parole. Even where a liberty interest is found, the Court has held that a Parole Board formal hearing, which allowed the prisoner to insure that the records before the Board were accurate and to present evidence on his own behalf, satisfied the requirements of procedural due process.[559]

Revocation of parole also has been considered to be a "deprivation of liberty" protected by the European Convention and thus subject to judicial oversight. The leading case is *Weeks v. U.K.*,[560] in which a seventeen-year-old pleaded guilty to armed robbery, assaulting a police officer and being in the unlawful possession of a firearm. With respect to the first offence, he was sentenced to life imprisonment; for the second and third offenses he received 2 and 3 years' imprisonment respectively, all sentences to run concurrently.

---

[554]*See* Board of Pardons v. Allen, 107 S.Ct. 2415 (1987).

[555]Morrissey v. Brewer, 408 U.S. 471 (1972).

[556]Greenholtz v. Inmates of Nebraska Penal and Correctional Complex, 442 U.S. 1 (1979).

[557]*Supra* note 555, at 487–90.

[558]*Supra* note 556, at 12.

[559]*Id.* at 14–15.

[560]App. No. 9787/82, Eur. Court H.R., Judgment of 2 Mar. 1987, Ser. A No. 114.

It emerged that the applicant had committed the robbery [with a starting pistol loaded with blanks] because he wanted to pay back £3 which he owed his mother, who had told him that morning to find lodgings elsewhere. . . .

In passing sentence, Mr. Justice Thesiger said:

> ". . . [T]he facts of the offence and the evidence of the character and disposition of the accused . . . satisfy me that . . . he is a very dangerous young man. . . . I think an indeterminate sentence is the right sentence for somebody of this age, of this character and disposition, who is attracted to this form of conduct. That leaves the matter with the Secretary of State who can release him if and when those who have been watching him and examining him believe that with the passage of years he has become responsible. . . . "

Mr. Weeks applied for leave to appeal against the sentence to the Court of Appeal (Criminal Division) which . . . dismissed the application. . . . in the following terms:

> . . . . "At first sight a sentence of life imprisonment, particularly having regard to his age, sounds terrible, but when the factors to which reference has been made are considered it will be seen that this is really in mercy to the boy and will perhaps enable him to be released much sooner than if a long term of imprisonment had been imposed, which was the only other alternative.". . .

[Following his release on parole in March 1976, Weeks was convicted of several minor offenses, including burglary (stealing a sweater from a beach house), driving while uninsured and without a licence, possession of an air pistol, damaging a police blanket, and theft of some alcohol; his parole was revoked in June 1977.]

[T]he Government argued that the applicant's recall to prison in 1977 had not deprived him of his liberty because both his liberty and his right to liberty had been taken away from him for the rest of his life by virtue of the sentence of life imprisonment imposed on him in 1966. . . . The Government drew a distinction between liberty, properly understood, and a life prisoner being permitted to live on licence outside prison. In the latter case, the Government explained, the prisoner was still serving his sentence, albeit outside prison as a result of a privilege granted to him by the Home Secretary, but his right to liberty had not been restored to him. . . .

The Court is not convinced by such reasoning. . . .

Whether Mr. Weeks regained his "liberty", for the purposes

of Article 5 of the Convention, when released on licence in March 1976 is a question of fact, depending upon the actual circumstances of the regime to which he was subject. . . . The freedom enjoyed by a life prisoner, such as Mr. Weeks, released on licence is thus more circumscribed in law and more precarious than the freedom enjoyed by the ordinary citizen. Nevertheless, the restrictions to which Mr. Weeks' freedom outside prison was subject under the law are not sufficient to prevent its being qualified as a state of "liberty" for the purposes of Article 5. Hence, when recalling Mr. Weeks to prison in 1977, the Home Secretary was ordering his removal from an actual state of liberty, albeit one enjoyed in law as a privilege and not as of right, to a state of custody. . . .

It was not contested that Mr. Weeks' re-detention as from 30 June 1977 was in accordance with a procedure prescribed by English law and otherwise lawful under English law. . . .

In the absence of sufficient medical evidence justifying an order sending him to a mental institution, the only means available under the British sentencing machinery to achieve this purpose [of an indefinite sentence] was a life sentence. In substance, Mr. Weeks was being put at the disposal of the State because he needed continued supervision in custody for an unforeseeable length of time and, as a corollary, periodic reassessment in order to ascertain the most appropriate manner of dealing with him. . . .

[T]he formal legal connection between Mr. Weeks' conviction in 1966 and his recall to prison some ten years later is not on its own sufficient to justify the contested detention under Article 5 §1(a). . . .

[However, in view of Weeks'] unstable, disturbed and aggressive behaviour, there were grounds for the Home Secretary to have considered that the applicant's continued liberty would constitute a danger to the public and to himself. The Minister's decision to re-detain remained within the bounds of the margin of appreciation available to the responsible national authorities; it cannot be regarded as arbitrary or unreasonable in terms of the objectives of the sentence imposed on Mr. Weeks. . . .

In the Court's view, therefore, a sufficient connection, for the purposes of sub-paragraph (a) of Article 5 §1, existed between [Weeks'] conviction in 1966 and his recall to prison in 1977. . . .

[Weeks additionally complained that he did not have the opportunity to challenge his re-detention through proceedings which were compatible with article 5(4).]

Article 5 §4 does not guarantee a right to judicial control of such scope as to empower the "court", on all aspects of the case, including questions of expediency, to substitute its own discretion for that of the decision-making authority. The review should, however, be wide enough to bear on those conditions which, according to the Convention, are essential for the lawful detention of a person subject to the special kind of deprivation of liberty ordered against Mr. Weeks. . . .

The "court" referred to in Article 5 §4 does not necessarily have to be a court of law of the classic kind integrated within the standard judicial machinery of the country. . . .

There is nothing to preclude a specialised body such as the Parole Board being considered as a "court" within the meaning of Article 5 §4. . . . [On the facts of the case, the Court found that the Parole Board was sufficiently independent (even though its members were appointed by the Home Secretary) and impartial to fall within the requirements of article 5(4).]

[However,] the Board's functions are without doubt purely advisory, both in law and in substance, as regards the periodic review that it carries out in relation to the question of the possible release on licence of a detained person serving a sentence of life imprisonment. . . . Quite apart from any consideration of procedural guarantees, the Board therefore lacks the power of decision required by Article 5 §4 when dealing with this category of case. . . .

The Board deals with individual cases on consideration of the documents supplied to it by the Home Secretary and of any reports, information or interviews with the individual concerned it has itself called for. The prisoner is entitled to make representations with respect to his recall, not only in writing to the Board but also orally to a member of the Local Review Committee. The individual is free to take legal advice in preparing such representations. Furthermore, he must be sufficiently informed of the reasons for his recall in order to enable him to make sensible representations.

Whilst these safeguards are not negligible, there remains a certain procedural weakness in the case of a recalled prisoner. Thus, . . . the duty on the Board to act fairly, as required under English law by the principles of natural justice, does not entail an entitlement to full disclosure of the adverse material which the Board has in its possession. The procedure followed does not therefore allow proper participation of the individual adversely affected by the contested decision, this being one of the principal guarantees of a judicial procedure for the purposes of the Convention, and cannot therefore be regarded as judicial in character.

. . .

Consequently, neither in relation to consideration of Mr. Weeks' recall to prison in 1977 nor in relation to periodic examination of his detention with a view to release on licence can the Parole Board be regarded as satisfying the requirements of Article 5 §4. . . .[561]

The Commission reached a similar conclusion in the context of the administrative re-detention of recidivists, holding that article 5(4) requires the possibility of judicial challenge to any such detention.[562] The European Court of Human Rights has found that withdrawal of substantial remission time (i.e., early release on parole) constitutes a criminal rather than disciplinary proceeding and therefore gives rise to the right to a hearing by a fair and independent tribunal and other defense rights.[63]

> The Court . . . does not find that the distinction between privilege and right is of great assistance to it for the present purposes; what is more important is that the practice of granting remission—whereby a prisoner will be set free on the estimated date for release given to him at the outset of his sentence, unless remission has been forfeited in disciplinary proceedings—creates in him a legitimate expectation that he will recover his liberty before the end of his term of imprisonment. . . .
>
> [T]he forfeiture of remission which [the applicant] risked incurring and the forfeiture actually awarded involved such serious consequences as regards the length of his detention [in this case, the potential loss of remission was nearly three years and the actual loss ordered 570 days] that these penalties have to be regarded, for Convention purposes, as "criminal". By causing detention to continue for substantially longer than would otherwise have been the case, the sanction came close to, even if it did not technically constitute, deprivation of liberty and the object and purpose of the Convention require that the imposition of a measure of such gravity should be accompanied by the guarantees of Article 6.[564]

---

[561]*Id.* at paras. 10-15, 39-69; citations and cross-references omitted.

[562]Van Droogenbroeck v. Belgium, *supra* note 105. *Also see* Christinet v. Switzerland, *supra* note 221 (no violation on the facts of the case, where redetention was not discretionary and administrative law appeal was possible).

[563]Campbell & Fell v. U.K., *supra* note 243.

[564]*Id.* at para. 72. The Court went on to find that the board which heard the case was sufficiently "independent" and "impartial" and that "there were sufficient reasons of public order and security" to justify excluding the press and public from the proceedings. However, it found a violation of article 6 insofar as the board's decision was never made public, and there was no right to be represented by legal counsel.

This case would appear to limit an earlier decision by the European Commission, in which a period of 80 days actual and up to six months possible loss of remission was found to be insufficient, by itself, to bring the proceedings within the range of "criminal" rather than "disciplinary". "[L]oss of remission does not constitute deprivation of liberty. A prisoner, unlike a person doing military service, is deprived of his liberty for the whole of his sentence; any remission of that sentence for good behaviour is mere privilege and loss of that privilege does not alter the original basis for detention."[565]

U.S. courts also have held that procedural safeguards must be followed when prison officials deny statutorily authorized "good time", including the right to notice of the disciplinary charges 24 hours before a hearing, a written statement of the evidence on which a decision is based and the reasons for the action taken, and the right to call witnesses and present evidence (assuming the safety and the goals of the prison are not jeopardized).[566] Most courts also have required that procedural safeguards be included in any disciplinary proceeding which could result in punitive confinement.[567]

Other Rights

Prison conditions, which are considered under international jurisprudence to fall within the prohibition against torture and other ill-treatment, are discussed *supra* at 63–70. Other normal incidents of imprisonment—such as requirements to wear prison clothing,[568] searches,[569] surveillance by prison guards,[570] and restrictions on visits[571]—have generally been upheld by international monitoring bodies.

The Thirteenth Amendment allows involuntary servitude as a punishment for criminal acts, and international norms similarly exclude prison

---

[565]Kiss v. U.K., App. No. 6224/73, Eur. Comm. H.R., dec. on admissibility of 16 Dec. 1976, 20 Y.B. EUR. CONV. ON HUMAN RIGHTS 156.

[566]Wolff v. McDonnell, 418 U.S. 539, 563–71.

[567]*See, e.g.*, Finney v. Arkansas Board of Corrections, 505 F.2d 194 (8th Cir. 1974).

[568]*See* McFeeley et al. v. U.K., App. No. 8217/78, Eur. Comm. H.R., dec. on admissibility of 15 May 1980, 20 Dec. & Rep. 44 ("H Block" protest in Northern Ireland).

[569]*Id.*

[570]*Id.*

[571]*Id. Also see, e.g.*, Bonzi v. Switzerland, App. No. 7854/77, Eur. Comm. H.R., dec. on admissibility of 12 July 1978, 12 Dec. & Rep. 185 (solitary confinement and restriction on visits for one month); X v. Belgium, App. No. 4400/70, Eur. Comm. H.R., dec. on admissibility of 24 July 1970 (unpublished), *excerpts reprinted in* 3 STRASBOURG DIGEST 123 (restrictions were "the normal consequences of detention").

labor from prohibitions against slavery or forced labor.[572] All the relevant international human rights instruments except the European Convention specifically prohibit requiring prisoners to work for private parties; the European Commission of Human Rights has upheld such contract labor—which is common in Europe—as within the "work required to be done in the ordinary course of detention" permitted under the Convention.[573] The European Court of Human Rights also has upheld requiring a prisoner to work in order to comply with a "savings" requirement "calculated to assist him in reintegrating himself into society".[574]

[572]*See* CivPol, art. 8(3(b); American, art. 6(3)(a); European, art. 4(3)(a); Convention Concerning Forced or Compulsory Labour (ILO No. 29), *adopted* 28 June 1930, *entered into force* 1 May 1932, 39 U.N.T.S. 55, art. 2(2)(c).

[573]*See* Detained Persons v. F.R.G., Apps. Nos. 3134, 3172, 3188 & 3206/67, Eur. Comm. H.R., dec. on admissibility of 6 Apr. 1968, 11 Y.B. EUR. CONV. ON HUMAN RIGHTS 528.

[574]Van Droogenbroeck v. Belgium, *supra* note 105; *also see* De Wilde, Ooms & Versyp v. Belgium ("Vagrancy Cases"), *supra* note 202.

CONCLUDING OBSERVATIONS

Direct comparisons of the jurisprudence of different legal systems is difficult at best, and comparison of a domestic legal order with an international regime is no less so. Certain aspects of U.S. criminal procedure, such as the use of substantive due process to extend most of the protections of the Bill of Rights to the states, have no counterpart in interpreting international treaties which protect rights directly.

Another significant difference applicable to comparisons of U.S. law with international (as opposed to foreign) law is the role of international tribunals. The task of international human rights bodies is not to substitute their judgment for that of domestic courts, but only to ensure that the basic rights guaranteed under international human rights treaties are respected. One of the basic international norms with which the present work is concerned—that every criminal accused has the right to a fair trial—is result-oriented, and the means by which that result is obtained are left largely to the discretion of the individual country concerned.

Nevertheless, the results (and many of the mechanisms) guaranteed under international law are very similar to those found in U.S. law and practice. A former President of the European Commission of Human Rights described the basic requirements for the administration of criminal justice under the European Convention of Human Rights, excluding "incidental matter," as follows:

> An individual may be arrested and detained on the reasonable suspicion that he has committed an offence; he must then be brought promptly before a judicial officer, and must also be brought to trial for the offence within a reasonable time or released pending trial, it may be on bail or on some other condition to secure his appearance; and, once charged, he must tried within a reasonable time.[575]

---

[575]J. FAWCETT, *supra* note 169, at 85. Fawcett goes on to note that "the confused distribution of the ideas involved [in arts. 5 and 6 of the European Convention] . . . make these provisions among the most difficult in the Convention to construe and apply." *Id.*

This surely corresponds in general to U.S. standards, although the practice of both international and domestic lawyers is largely spent refining the "incidental matter" omitted from this brief description.

Primarily as a result of the need for greater generality at the international level, the procedural guarantees available to an accused in the United States are undoubtedly more extensive than those guaranteed internationally. However, international law may offer at least a few advances over present U.S. law, such as, e.g., the broader prohibition against "inhuman or degrading treatment or punishment,"[576] the more restrictive use of the death penalty,[577] and the provision in several human rights instruments that an accused benefit from any reduction in penalty which might have occurred between the time the offense was committed and the trial.[578]

Any survey of international norms also confirms that some components considered fundamental in the American system of criminal justice—such as the right to trial by jury, use of the exclusionary rule, plea-bargaining, and even the full scope of the privilege against self-incrimination—are not universal, even though they may have become essential in the particular approach to criminal procedure which has developed in the United States. At the same time, frequent references by international judges to U.S. jurisprudence reflect the contribution that American concepts of due process have made to international human rights.[579]

Finally, it should be emphasized that international human rights norms represent the *minimum* standards applicable to detention and criminal proceedings. Thus, it should be expected that broader guarantees, designed to ensure the rights of an accused as well as serving the interests of justice, would be found in countries with a well-developed legal system, such as the United States.

Both American and international norms seek to promote individual liberty and social justice, and the balance between these sometimes contradictory goals can only be maintained with vigilance. International human rights norms against arbitrary detention and requiring a fair trial parallel concepts which are basic to the U.S. system of criminal justice, and it is essential that both of these values be kept in mind as the mechanisms intended to implement them change.

---

[576]*See* discussion *supra* at 59–63.

[577]*See* discussion *supra* at 71–77.

[578]*E.g.*, CivPol, art. 15; American, art. 9.

[579]*See* Lester, *The Overseas Trade in the American Bill of Rights*, 88 COL. L. REV. 537, 544–47 (1988).

Just as criminal justice at the state level in the United States has become a matter of fundamental constitutional concern in recent decades, so are minimum guarantees gradually being established at the international level. It is hoped that the United States will expand its own protections where necessary to keep pace with internationally recognized rights, as well as increase its contribution to defining those rights by ratifying the major human rights treaties and participating in the process of their interpretation.[580]

---

[580]One noted European human rights lawyer has observed with regret "the continued isolation of American constitutional law from international human rights law" and suggests that "it is . . . a misfortune for the United States itself, not only in diminishing American influence overseas, but also in separating American constitutional law from the ideas and values of other advanced democratic nations and their courts." *Id.* at 560, 561.

APPENDIX I

Documentary Sources for International Cases and Materials

Few American lawyers are familiar with international human rights decisions and cases, but most may be obtained in major law libraries or directly from the relevant international organization. Nevertheless, some understanding of the basic reporting systems and publications available will facilitate the task of researching decisions of interest to the individual practitioner or professor.

In addition to the source cited in the text, R. Lillich, *International Human Rights Instruments* (1988), the most important international treaties and other instruments may be found in, e.g., I. Brownlie, *Basic Documents on Human Rights* (2d ed. 1981); United Nations, *A Compilation of International Instruments*, UN Sales No. E.88.XIV.1 (1988); and House Comm. on Foreign Affairs, *Human Rights Documents* (Comm. Print 1983).

United Nations and Human Rights Committee

As noted in the text, the most important global instrument concerning human rights is the Covenant on Civil and Political Rights, which has been ratified by over 85 countries. Implementation the Covenant is overseen by the Human Rights Committee, an independent body of eighteen experts, elected by the parties to the Covenant, which meets three times per year.

The "views" of the Committee on individual cases filed under the Optional Protocol to the Covenant, as well as the "general comments" it adopts on particular rights or issues, are found in the annual *Report of the Human Rights Committee* to the UN General Assembly. These reports are issued as supplements to the General Assembly's Official Records and should be readily available; each is identified by a UN document number, e.g., UN Doc. A/42/40.[1]

Since 1986, the Committee has published an annual two-volume *Yearbook of the Human Rights Committee*, which includes the Committee's annual reports to the General Assembly, the periodic reports by countries filed under article 40 of the covenant, and the summary records of the Committee's discussions of these reports. While there is a lag of several years between the original reports and the *Yearbook*, the latter does offer a useful alternative source. Most of the Committee's opinions in individual cases through 1982 have been reprinted in *Selected Decisions under the Optional Protocol*, UN Sales No. E.84.XIV.2 (1985), and a second volume of *Selected Decisions* is expected to be published in 1989.

Other UN materials which may be of interest are likely to be found as separate UN publications (identified by a UN Sales No. and available from UN libraries and bookstores) or as documents of the UN Commission on Human Rights and its Sub-Commission on Prevention of Discrimination and Protection of Minorities. The latter are identified, respectively, by UN document designations of E/CN.4/– or E/CN.4/Sub.2/–.

UN documents are available from the United Nations, Sales Section, New York, NY 10017, or the Centre for Human Rights, United Nations, Palais des Nations, 1211 Geneva 10, Switzerland.

European Convention on Human Rights

As evidenced by the number of citations in the present work, the European system for implementing the European Convention on Human Rights has a well-developed reporting system that by now includes thousands of cases. All cases are first heard by the European Commission of Human Rights; those which are decided on the merits by the Commission may be appealed (by the Commission itself or a concerned state) to the European Court of Human Rights. Each case is identified by a number which indicates its chronological place in the cases registered with the Commission and the year of registration, e.g., 10868/84, as well as by the name(s) or initials of the applicant.

The Commission's decisions on admissibility (jurisdiction) and its final reports on each case are published in three forms. At the time of decision, a soft-cover slip opinion is issued; most (although not all) decisions are additionally reported in the periodic *Decisions and Reports* (cited herein as "Dec. & Rep.", replacing the previous *Collection of Decisions*, "Coll. Dec."), which is the basic reporting system for the Commission; the most significant cases are reprinted in the *Yearbook of the European Convention on Human Rights*, published by the Council of

[1]"A" designates a document of the General Assembly; "42" indicates the number of the General Assembly session (the forty-second session was held in 1987); and "40" is the number, which changes annually, of the supplement comprising the Committee's report.

Europe. The *Yearbook* also contains information on the application of the Convention in domestic law in the various countries of Europe.

Judgments of the European Court of Human Rights also are issued initially as soft-cover slip opinions; these are subsequently published in more permanent form as Series A (judgments) and Series B (pleadings, etc.) of the Court's publications. The most significant judgments also may be reprinted in the *Yearbook*. The Court assigns a new, more complicated number to each case it hears, but cases are more generally identified simply by the name of the applicant.

Selected decisions of both the Commission and Court also are published in the *European Human Rights Reporter*, which includes relevant domestic cases, as well.

The texts of the Convention and its protocols, including rules of procedure, the current status of ratifications, and other information, are contained in the Council of Europe publication *Collected Texts*, which is updated periodically.

Documents of the European Commission and Court are available from the Council of Europe, 67000 Strasbourg Cedex, France.

American Convention on Human Rights

Documents of the Inter-American system combine features of both the UN and European systems. Decisions of the Inter-American Commission on Human Rights are identified by a case number, followed by the name of the country concerned, and are published in its *Annual Report* to the General Assembly of the Organization of American States (which is based in Washington, DC). An *Inter-American Yearbook on Human Rights* has appeared sporadically and includes reprints of Commission decisions and reports, as well as summaries of recent developments. The Commission's reports on the situation of human rights in individual countries, which often contain detailed legal analyses of particular issues, are issued in soft-cover format as they are adopted.

Judgments and decisions of the Inter-American Court on Human Rights are published in a form comparable to that of the European Court of Human Rights, i.e., each judgment and the corresponding pleadings, oral arguments, and other documents considered in the case are published separately. As in Europe, cases are numbered consecutively, in order of judgment. The Court also submits an *Annual Report* to the OAS General Assembly, which summarizes the Court's activities and may reprint important decisions.

OAS documents are available from the Organization of American States, Department of Publications, Washington, DC 20006; the Inter-American Commission on Human Rights, at the same address; or from the Secretariat of the Inter-American Court of Human Rights, San Jose, Costa Rica.

APPENDIX II

Excerpts from Selected Texts

Constitution of the United States

Article I, § 9, cl. 2

The Privilege of the Writ of Habeas Corpus shall not be suspended, unless when in Cases of Rebellion or Invasion the public Safety may require it.

Article I, § 10, cl. 1

No State shall enter into any Treaty, Alliance, or Confederation;. . . .

Article I, § 10, cl. 3

No State shall, without the Consent of Congress, . . . enter into any Agreement or Compact with another State, or with a foreign Power,. . . .

Article II, § 2, cl. 2

He [the President] shall have Power, by and with the Advice and Consent of the Senate, to make Treaties, provided two thirds of the Senators present concur; . . .

Article VI, cl. 2

This Constitution, and the Laws of the United States which shall be made in Pursuance thereof; and all Treaties made, or which shall be made, under the Authority of the United States, shall be the supreme Law of the Land; and the Judges in every State shall be bound thereby, any Thing in the Constitution or Laws of any State to the Contrary notwithstanding.

Amend. IV

The right of the people to be secure in their persons, houses, papers, and effects, against unreasonable searches and seizures, shall not be violated, and no Warrants shall issue, but upon probable cause, supported by Oath or affirmation, and particularly describing the place to be searched, and the persons or things to be seized.

Amend. V

No person shall be held to answer for a capital, or otherwise infamous crime, unless on a presentment or indictment of a Grand Jury, . . . nor shall any person be subject for the same offence to be twice put in jeopardy of life or limb; nor shall be compelled in any criminal case to be a witness against himself, nor be deprived of life, liberty, or property, without due process of law; nor shall private property be taken for public use without just compensation.

Amend. VI

In all criminal prosecutions, the accused shall enjoy the right to a speedy and public trial, by an impartial jury of the State and district wherein the crime shall have been committed, which district shall have been previously ascertained by law, and to be informed of the nature and cause of the accusation; to be confronted with the witnesses against him; to have compulsory process for obtaining Witnesses in his favor, and to have the assistance of counsel for his defence.

Amend. VIII

Excessive bail shall not be required, nor excessive fines imposed, nor cruel and unusual punishments inflicted.

Amend. XIII, § 1

Neither slavery nor involuntary servitude, except as a punishment for crime whereof the party shall have been duly convicted, shall exist within the United States, or any place subject to their jurisdiction.

Amend. XIV, § 1

. . . . No State shall make or enforce any law which shall abridge the privileges or immunities of citizens of the United States; nor shall any State deprive any person of life, liberty, or property, without due process of law; nor deny to any person within its jurisdiction the equal protection of the laws.

Covenant on Civil and Political Rights

Article 6

1. Every human being has the inherent right to life. This right shall be protected by law. No one shall be arbitrarily deprived of his life.

2. In countries which have not abolished the death penalty, sentence of death may be imposed only for the most serious crimes in accordance with the law in force at the time of the commission of the crime. . . . The penalty can only be carried out pursuant to a final judgement rendered by a competent court. . . .

4. Anyone sentenced to death shall have the right to seek pardon or commutation of the sentence. Amnesty, pardon or commutation of the sentence of death may be granted in all cases.

5. Sentence of death shall not be imposed for crimes committed by persons below eighteen years of age and shall not be carried out on pregnant women.

6. Nothing in this article shall be invoked to delay or to prevent the abolition of capital punishment. . . .

Article 7

No one shall be subjected to torture or to cruel, inhuman or degrading treatment or punishment. In particular, no one shall be subjected without his free consent to medical or scientific experimentation.

Article 9

1. Everyone has the right to liberty and security of person. No one shall be subjected to arbitrary arrest or detention. No one shall be deprived of his liberty except on such grounds and in accordance with such procedures as are established by law.

2. Anyone who is arrested shall be informed, at the time of arrest, of the reasons for his arrest and shall be promptly informed of any charges against him.

3. Anyone arrested or detained on a criminal charge shall be brought promptly before a judge or other officer authorized by law to exercise judicial power and shall be entitled to trial within a reasonable time or to release. It shall not be the general rule that persons awaiting trial shall be detained in custody, but release may be subject to guarantees to appear for trial, at any other stage of the judicial proceedings, and, should occasion arise, for execution of the judgement.

4. Anyone who is deprived of his liberty by arrest or detention

shall be entitled to take proceedings before a court, in order that that court may decide without delay on the lawfulness of his detention and order his release if the detention is not lawful.

5. Anyone who has been the victim of unlawful arrest or detention shall have an enforceable right to compensation.

Article 10

1. All persons deprived of their liberty shall be treated with humanity and with respect for the inherent dignity of the human person.

2. a. Accused persons shall, save in exceptional circumstances, be segregated from convicted persons and shall be subject to separate treatment appropriate to their status as unconvicted persons;

b. Accused juvenile persons shall be separated from adults and brought as speedily as possible for adjudication.

3. The penitentiary system shall comprise treatment of prisoners the essential aim of which shall be their reformation and social rehabilitation. Juvenile offenders shall be segregated from adults and be accorded treatment appropriate to their age and legal status.

Article 14

1. All persons shall be equal before the courts and tribunals. In the determination of any criminal charge against him, or of his rights and obligations in a suit at law, everyone shall be entitled to a fair and public hearing by a competent, independent and impartial tribunal established by law. The press and the public may be excluded from all or part of a trial for reasons of morals, public order (*ordre public*) or national security in a democratic society, or when the interest of the private lives of the parties so requires, or to the extent strictly necessary in the opinion of the court in special circumstances where publicity would prejudice the interests of justice; but any judgement rendered in a criminal case or in a suit at law shall be made public except where the interest of juvenile persons otherwise requires or the proceedings concern matrimonial disputes or the guardianship of children.

2. Everyone charged with a criminal offence shall have the right to be presumed innocent until proved guilty according to law.

3. In the determination of any criminal charge against him, everyone shall be entitled to the following minimum guarantees, in full equality:

a. To be informed promptly and in detail in a language which he understands of the nature and cause of the charge against him;

b. To have adequate time and facilities for the preparation of his defence and to communicate with counsel of his own choosing;

c. To be tried without undue delay;

d. To be tried in his presence, and to defend himself in person or through legal assistance of his own choosing; to be informed, if he does not have legal assistance, of this right; and to have legal assistance assigned to him, in any case where the interests of justice so require, and without payment by him in any such case if he does not have sufficient means to pay for it;

e. To examine, or have examined, the witnesses against him and to obtain the attendance and examination of witnesses on his behalf under the same conditions as witnesses against him;

f. To have the free assistance of an interpreter if he cannot understand or speak the language used in court;

g. Not to be compelled to testify against himself or to confess guilt.

4. In the case of juvenile persons, the procedure shall be such as will take account of their age and the desirability of promoting their rehabilitation.

5. Everyone convicted of a crime shall have the right to his conviction and sentence being reviewed by a higher tribunal according to law.

6. When a person has by a final decision been convicted of a criminal offence and when subsequently his conviction has been reversed or he has been pardoned on the ground that a new or newly discovered fact shows conclusively that there has been a miscarriage of justice, the person who has suffered punishment as a result of such conviction shall be compensated according to law, unless it is proved that the non-disclosure of the unknown fact in time is wholly or partly attributable to him.

7. No one shall be liable to be tried or punished again for an offence for which he has already been finally convicted or acquitted in accordance with the law and penal procedure of each country.

Article 15

No one shall be held guilty of any criminal offence on account of any act or omission which did not constitute a criminal offence, under national or international law, at the time when it was committed. Nor shall a heavier penalty be imposed than the one that was applicable at the time when the criminal offence was committed. If, subsequent to the commission of the offence, provision is made by law for the imposition of the lighter penalty, the offender shall benefit thereby.

2. Nothing in this article shall prejudice the trial and punishment of any person for any act or omission which, at the time when it was committed, was criminal according to the general principles of law recognized by the community of nations.

American Convention on Human Rights

Article 4

1. Every person has the right to have his life respected. This right shall be protected by law and, in general, from the moment of conception. No one shall be arbitrarily deprived of his life.

2. In countries that have not abolished the death penalty, it may be imposed only for the most serious crimes and pursuant to a final judgment rendered by a competent court and in accordance with a law establishing such punishment, enacted prior to the commission of the crime. The application of such punishment shall not be extended to crimes to which it does not presently apply.

3. The death penalty shall not be reestablished in states that have abolished it.

4. In no case shall capital punishment be inflicted for political offenses or related common crimes.

5. Capital punishment shall not be imposed upon persons who, at the time the crime was committed, were under 18 years of age or over 70 years of age; nor shall it be applied to pregnant women.

6. Every person condemned to death shall have the right to apply for amnesty, pardon, or commutation of sentence, which may be granted in all cases. Capital punishment shall not be imposed while such a petition is pending decision by the competent authority.

Article 5

1. Every person has the right to have his physical, mental, and moral integrity respected.

2. No one shall be subjected to torture or to cruel, inhuman, or degrading punishment or treatment. All persons deprived of

their liberty shall be treated with respect for the inherent dignity of the human person.

3. Punishment shall not be extended to any person other than the criminal.

4. Accused persons shall, save in exceptional circumstances, be segregated from convicted persons, and shall be subject to separate treatment appropriate to their status as unconvicted persons.

5. Minors while subject to criminal proceedings shall be separated from adults and brought before specialized tribunals, as speedily as possible, so that they may be treated in accordance with their status as minors.

6. Punishment consisting of deprivation of liberty shall have as an essential aim the reform and social readaptation of the prisoners.

Article 7

1. Every person has the right to personal liberty and security.

2. No one shall be deprived of his physical liberty except for the reasons and under the conditions established beforehand by the constitution of the State Party concerned or by a law established pursuant thereto.

3. No one shall be subject to arbitrary arrest or imprisonment.

4. Anyone who is detained shall be informed of the reasons for his detention and shall be promptly notified of the charge or charges against him.

5. Any person detained shall be brought promptly before a judge or other officer authorized by law to exercise judicial power and shall be entitled to trial within a reasonable time or to be released without prejudice to the continuation of the proceedings. His release may be subject to guarantees to assure his appearance for trial.

6. Anyone who is deprived of his liberty shall be entitled to recourse to a competent court, in order that the court may decide without delay on the lawfulness of his arrest or detention and order his release if the arrest or detention is unlawful. In States parties whose laws provide that anyone who believes himself to be threatened with deprivation of his liberty is entitled to recourse to a competent court in order that it may decide on the lawfulness of such threat, this remedy may not be restricted or abolished. The interested party or another person in his behalf is entitled to seek these remedies.

7. No one shall be detained for debt. This principle shall not limit the orders of a competent judicial authority issued for nonfulfillment of duties of support.

Article 8

1. Every person has the right to a hearing, with due guarantees and within a reasonable time, by a competent, independent and impartial tribunal, previously established by law, in the substantiation of any accusation of a criminal nature made against him or for the determination of his rights and obligations of a civil, labor, fiscal, or any other nature.

2. Every person accused of a criminal offence has the right to be presumed innocent so long as his guilt has not been proven according to law. During the proceedings, every person is entitled, with full equality, to the following minimum guarantees:

a. the right of the accused to be assisted without charge by a translator or interpreter, if he does not understand or does not speak the language of the tribunal or court;

b. prior notification in detail to the accused of the charges against him;

c. adequate time and means for the preparation of his defense;

d. the right of the accused to defend himself personally or to be assisted by legal counsel of his own choosing, and to communicate freely and privately with his counsel;

e. the inalienable right to be assisted by counsel provided by the state, paid or not as the domestic law provides, if the accused does not defend himself personally or engage his own counsel within the time period established by law;

f. the right of the defense to examine witnesses present in the court and to obtain the appearance, as witnesses, of experts or other persons who may throw light on the facts;

g. the right not to be compelled to be a witness against himself or to plead guilty; and

h. the right to appeal the judgment to a higher court.

3. A confession of guilt by the accused shall be valid only if it is made without coercion of any kind.

4. An accused person acquitted by a nonappealable judgment shall not be subjected to a new trial for the same cause.

5. Criminal proceedings shall be public, except insofar as may be necessary to protect the interests of justice.

Article 9

No one shall be convicted of any act or omission that did not constitute a criminal offense, under the applicable law, at the time it was committed. A heavier penalty shall not be imposed than the one that was applicable at the time the criminal offense was committed. If subsequent to the commission of the offense the law provides for the imposition of a lighter punishment, the guilty person shall benefit therefrom.

Article 10

Every person has the right to be compensated in accordance with the law in the event he has been sentenced by a final judgment through a miscarriage of justice.

European Convention on Human Rights

Article 3

No one shall be subjected to torture or to inhuman or degrading treatment or punishment.

Article 5

1. Everyone has the right to liberty and security of person.
No one shall be deprived of his liberty save in the following cases and in accordance with a procedure described by law:

a. the lawful detention of a person after conviction by a competent court;

b. the lawful arrest or detention of a person for non-compliance with the lawful order of a court or in order to secure the fulfilment of any obligation prescribed by law;

c. the lawful arrest or detention of a person effected for the purpose of bringing him before the competent legal authority on reasonable suspicion of having committed an offence or when it is reasonably considered necessary to prevent his committing an offence or fleeing after having done so;

d. the detention of a minor by lawful order for the purpose of educational supervision or his lawful detention for the purpose of bringing him before the competent legal authority;

e. the lawful detention of persons for the prevention of the spreading of infectious diseases, of persons of unsound mind,. alcoholics or drug addicts or vagrants;

f. the lawful arrest or detention of a person to prevent his effecting an unauthorised entry into the country or of a person against whom action is being taken with a view to deportation or extradition.

2. Everyone who is arrested shall be informed promptly, in a

language which he understands, of the reasons for his arrest and of any charge against him.

3. Everyone arrested or detained in accordance with the provisions of paragraph 1(c) of this Article shall be brought promptly before a judge or other officer authorised by law to exercise judicial power and shall be entitled to trial within a reasonable time or to release pending trial. Release may be conditioned by guarantees to appear for trial.

4. Everyone who is deprived of his liberty by arrest or detention shall be entitled to take proceedings by which the lawfulness of his detention shall be decided speedily by a court and his release ordered if the detention is not lawful.

5. Everyone who has been the victim of arrest or detention in contravention of the provisions of this Article shall have an enforceable right to compensation.

Article 6

1. In the determination of his civil rights and obligations or of any criminal charge against him, everyone is entitled to a fair and public hearing within a reasonable time by an independent and impartial tribunal established by law. Judgment shall be pronounced publicly but the press and public may be excluded from all or part of the trial in the interests of morals, public order or national security in a democratic society, where the interests of juveniles or the protection of the private life of the parties so require, or to the extent strictly necessary in the opinion of the court in special circumstances where publicity would prejudice the interests of justice.

2. Everyone charged with a criminal offence shall be presumed innocent until proved guilty according to law.

3. Everyone charged with a criminal offence has the following minimum rights:

a. to be informed promptly, in a language which he understands and in detail, of the nature and cause of the accusation against him;

b. to have adequate time and facilities for the preparation of his defence;

c. to defend himself in person or through legal assistance of his own choosing or, if he has not sufficient means to pay for legal assistance, to be given it free when the interests of justice so require;

d. to examine or have examined witnesses against him and to obtain the attendance and examination of witnesses on his behalf under the same conditions as witnesses against him;

e. to have the free assistance of an interpreter if he cannot understand or speak the language used in court.

Article 7

1. No one shall be held guilty of any criminal offence on account of any act or omission which did not constitute a criminal offence under national or international law at the time when it was committed. Nor shall a heavier penalty be imposed than the one that was applicable at the time the criminal offence was committed.

2. This Article shall not prejudice the trial and punishment of any person for any act or omission which, at the time when it was committed, was criminal according to the general principles of law recognised by civilised nations.

African Charter on Human and Peoples' Rights

Article 4

Human beings are inviolable. Every human being shall be entitled to respect for his life and the integrity of his person. No one may be arbitrarily deprived of this right.

Article 5

Every individual shall have the right to the respect of the dignity inherent in a human being and to the recognition of his legal status. All forms of exploitation and degradation of man, particularly slavery, slave trade, torture, cruel, inhuman or degrading punishment and treatment shall be prohibited.

Article 6

Every individual shall have the right to liberty and to the security of his person. No one may be deprived of his freedom except for reasons and conditions previously laid down by law. In particular, no one may be arbitrarily arrested or detained.

Article 7

1. Every individual shall have the right to have his cause heard. This comprises:

a. the right to an appeal to competent national organs against acts violating his fundamental rights as recognized and guaranteed by conventions, laws, regulations and customs in force;

b. the right to be presumed innocent until proved guilty by a competent court or tribunal;

c. the right to defence, including the right to be defended by counsel of his choice;

d. the right to be tried within a reasonable time by an impartial court or tribunal.

2. No one may be condemned for an act or omission which did not constitute a legally punishable offence at the time it was committed. No penalty may be inflicted for an offence for which no provision was made at the time it was committed. Punishment is personal and can be imposed only on the offender.